LaTeX in 157 minutes

A catalogue record for this book is available from the Hong Kong Public Libraries.

Published by Samurai Media Limited.

Email: info@samuraimedia.org

ISBN 978-988-14436-2-5

Background Cover Image by https://www.flickr.com/people/webtreatsetc/

Thank you!

Much of the material used in this introduction comes from an Austrian introduction to LaTeX 2.09 written in German by:

Hubert Partl   `<partl@mail.boku.ac.at>`
 Zentraler Informatikdienst der Universität für Bodenkultur Wien

Irene Hyna   `<Irene.Hyna@bmwf.ac.at>`
 Bundesministerium für Wissenschaft und Forschung Wien

Elisabeth Schlegl   `<noemail>`
 in Graz

If you are interested in the German document, you can find a version updated for LaTeX 2_ε by Jörg Knappen at `CTAN://info/lshort/german`

The following individuals helped with corrections, suggestions and material to improve this paper. They put in a big effort to help me get this document into its present shape. I would like to sincerely thank all of them. Naturally, all the mistakes you'll find in this book are mine. If you ever find a word that is spelled correctly, it must have been one of the people below dropping me a line.

Eric Abrahamsen, Lenimar Nunes de Andrade, Eilinger August, Rosemary Bailey, Barbara Beeton, Marc Bevand, Connor Blakey, Salvatore Bonaccorso, Pietro Braione, Friedemann Brauer, Markus Brühwiler, Jan Busa, David Carlisle, Neil Carter, Carl Cerecke, Mike Chapman, Pierre Chardaire, Xingyou Chen, Christopher Chin, Diego Clavadetscher, Wim van Dam, Benjamin Deschwanden Jan Dittberner, Michael John Downes, Matthias Dreier, David Dureisseix, Hans Ehrbar, Elliot, Rockrush Engch, William Faulk, Robin Fairbairns, Johan Falk, Jörg Fischer, Frank Fischli, Daniel Flipo, Frank, Mic Milic Frederickx, David Frey, Erik Frisk, Hans Fugal, Robert Funnell, Greg Gamble, Andy Goth, Cyril Goutte, Kasper B. Graversen, Arlo Griffiths, Alexandre Guimond, Neil Hammond, Christoph Hamburger, Rasmus Borup Hansen, Joseph Hilferty, Daniel Hirsbrunner, Martien Hulsen, Björn Hvittfeldt, Morten Høgholm, Werner Icking, Eric Jacoboni, Jakob, Alan Jeffrey, Martin Jenkins, Byron Jones, David Jones, Johannes-Maria Kaltenbach, Nils Kanning, Andrzej Kawalec, Christian Kern, Alain Kessi, Axel Kielhorn, Sander de Kievit, Kjetil Kjernsmo, Tobias Klauser, Jörg Knappen, Michael Koundouros, Matt Kraai, Tobias Krewer, Flori Lambrechts, Mike Lee, Maik Lehradt, Rémi Letot, Axel Liljencrantz, Jasper Loy, Johan Lundberg, Martin Maechler, Alexander Mai, Claus Malten, Kevin Van Maren, Pablo Markin, I. J. Vera Marún, Hendrik Maryns, Chris McCormack, Aleksandar S. Milosevic, Henrik Mitsch, Stefan M. Moser, Philipp Nagele, Richard Nagy, Manuel Oetiker, Urs Oswald, Hubert Partl, Marcelo Pasin, Martin Pfister, Lan Thuy Pham, Breno Pietracci, Demerson Andre Polli, Maksym Polyakov, Nikos Pothitos, John Refling, Mike Ressler, Brian Ripley, Kurt Rosenfeld, Bernd Rosenlecher, Chris Rowley, Young U. Ryu, Risto Saarelma, András Salamon, José Carlos Santos, Christopher Sawtell, Gilles Schintgen, Craig Schlenter, Hanspeter Schmid, Baron Schwartz, Jordi Serra i Solanich, Miles Spielberg, Susan Stewart, Matthieu Stigler, Geoffrey Swindale, Laszlo Szathmary, Boris Tobotras, Josef Tkadlec, Scott Veirs, Didier Verna, Carl-Gustav Werner, Fabian Wernli, Matthew Widmann, David Woodhouse, Chris York, Rick Zaccone, Fritz Zaucker, and Mikhail Zotov.

Preface

LaTeX [1] is a typesetting system that is very suitable for producing scientific and mathematical documents of high typographical quality. It is also suitable for producing all sorts of other documents, from simple letters to complete books. LaTeX uses TeX [2] as its formatting engine.

This short introduction describes LaTeX 2_ε and should be sufficient for most applications of LaTeX. Refer to [1, 3] for a complete description of the LaTeX system.

This introduction is split into 6 chapters:

Chapter 1 tells you about the basic structure of LaTeX 2_ε documents. You will also learn a bit about the history of LaTeX. After reading this chapter, you should have a rough understanding how LaTeX works.

Chapter 2 goes into the details of typesetting your documents. It explains most of the essential LaTeX commands and environments. After reading this chapter, you will be able to write your first documents.

Chapter 3 explains how to typeset formulae with LaTeX. Many examples demonstrate how to use one of LaTeX's main strengths. At the end of the chapter are tables listing all mathematical symbols available in LaTeX.

Chapter 4 explains indexes, bibliography generation and inclusion of EPS graphics. It introduces creation of PDF documents with pdfLaTeX and presents some handy extension packages.

Chapter 5 shows how to use LaTeX for creating graphics. Instead of drawing a picture with some graphics program, saving it to a file and then including it into LaTeX, you describe the picture and have LaTeX draw it for you.

Chapter 6 contains some potentially dangerous information about how to alter the standard document layout produced by LaTeX. It will tell you how to change things such that the beautiful output of LaTeX turns ugly or stunning, depending on your abilities.

It is important to read the chapters in order—the book is not that big, after all. Be sure to carefully read the examples, because a lot of the information is in the examples placed throughout the book.

LaTeX is available for most computers, from the PC and Mac to large UNIX and VMS systems. On many university computer clusters you will find that a LaTeX installation is available, ready to use. Information on how to access the local LaTeX installation should be provided in the *Local Guide* [5]. If you have problems getting started, ask the person who gave you this booklet. The scope of this document is *not* to tell you how to install and set up a LaTeX system, but to teach you how to write your documents so that they can be processed by LaTeX.

If you need to get hold of any LaTeX related material, have a look at one of the Comprehensive TeX Archive Network (CTAN) sites. The homepage is at `http://www.ctan.org`.

You will find other references to CTAN throughout the book, especially pointers to software and documents you might want to download. Instead of writing down complete urls, I just wrote `CTAN:` followed by whatever location within the CTAN tree you should go to.

If you want to run LaTeX on your own computer, take a look at what is available from `CTAN://systems`.

If you have ideas for something to be added, removed or altered in this document, please let me know. I am especially interested in feedback from LaTeX novices about which bits of this intro are easy to understand and which could be explained better.

Tobias Oetiker   `<tobi@oetiker.ch>`

OETIKER+PARTNER AG
Aarweg 15
4600 Olten
Switzerland

The current version of this document is available on
`CTAN://info/lshort`

Contents

List of Figures

List of Tables

Chapter 1

Things You Need to Know

The first part of this chapter presents a short overview of the philosophy and history of LATEX 2ε. The second part focuses on the basic structures of a LATEX document. After reading this chapter, you should have a rough knowledge of how LATEX works, which you will need to understand the rest of this book.

1.1 The Name of the Game

1.1.1 TEX

TEX is a computer program created by Donald E. Knuth [2]. It is aimed at typesetting text and mathematical formulae. Knuth started writing the TEX typesetting engine in 1977 to explore the potential of the digital printing equipment that was beginning to infiltrate the publishing industry at that time, especially in the hope that he could reverse the trend of deteriorating typographical quality that he saw affecting his own books and articles. TEX as we use it today was released in 1982, with some slight enhancements added in 1989 to better support 8-bit characters and multiple languages. TEX is renowned for being extremely stable, for running on many different kinds of computers, and for being virtually bug free. The version number of TEX is converging to π and is now at 3.141592653.

TEX is pronounced "Tech," with a "ch" as in the German word "Ach"[1] or in the Scottish "Loch." The "ch" originates from the Greek alphabet where X is the letter "ch" or "chi". TEX is also the first syllable of the Greek word τεχνική (technique). In an ASCII environment, TEX becomes TeX.

---

[1]In german there are actually two pronounciations for "ch" and one might assume that the soft "ch" sound from "Pech" would be a more appropriate. Asked about this, Knuth wrote in the German Wikipedia: *I do not get angry when people pronounce TEX in their favorite way ... and in Germany many use a soft ch because the X follows the vowel e, not the harder ch that follows the vowel a. In Russia, 'tex' is a very common word, pronounced 'tyekh'. But I believe the most proper pronunciation is heard in Greece, where you have the harsher ch of ach and Loch.*

1.1.2   LaTeX

LaTeX enables authors to typeset and print their work at the highest typographical quality, using a predefined, professional layout. LaTeX was originally written by Leslie Lamport [1]. It uses the TeX formatter as its typesetting engine. These days LaTeX is maintained by Frank Mittelbach.

LaTeX is pronounced "Lay-tech" or "Lah-tech." If you refer to LaTeX in an ASCII environment, you type LaTeX. LaTeX 2_ε is pronounced "Lay-tech two e" and typed LaTeX2e.

1.2   Basics

1.2.1   Author, Book Designer, and Typesetter

To publish something, authors give their typed manuscript to a publishing company. One of their book designers then decides the layout of the document (column width, fonts, space before and after headings, . . .). The book designer writes his instructions into the manuscript and then gives it to a typesetter, who typesets the book according to these instructions.

A human book designer tries to find out what the author had in mind while writing the manuscript. He decides on chapter headings, citations, examples, formulae, etc. based on his professional knowledge and from the contents of the manuscript.

In a LaTeX environment, LaTeX takes the role of the book designer and uses TeX as its typesetter. But LaTeX is "only" a program and therefore needs more guidance. The author has to provide additional information to describe the logical structure of his work. This information is written into the text as "LaTeX commands."

This is quite different from the WYSIWYG[2] approach that most modern word processors, such as *MS Word* or *LibreOffice*, take. With these applications, authors specify the document layout interactively while typing text into the computer. They can see on the screen how the final work will look when it is printed.

When using LaTeX it is not normally possible to see the final output while typing the text, but the final output can be previewed on the screen after processing the file with LaTeX. Then corrections can be made before actually sending the document to the printer.

1.2.2   Layout Design

Typographical design is a craft. Unskilled authors often commit serious formatting errors by assuming that book design is mostly a question of aesthetics—"If a document looks good artistically, it is well designed." But

---

[2]What you see is what you get.

as a document has to be read and not hung up in a picture gallery, the readability and understandability is much more important than the beautiful look of it. Examples:

- The font size and the numbering of headings have to be chosen to make the structure of chapters and sections clear to the reader.

- The line length has to be short enough not to strain the eyes of the reader, while long enough to fill the page beautifully.

With WYSIWYG systems, authors often generate aesthetically pleasing documents with very little or inconsistent structure. LaTeX prevents such formatting errors by forcing the author to declare the *logical* structure of his document. LaTeX then chooses the most suitable layout.

1.2.3 Advantages and Disadvantages

When people from the WYSIWYG world meet people who use LaTeX, they often discuss "the advantages of LaTeX over a normal word processor" or the opposite. The best thing to do when such a discussion starts is to keep a low profile, since such discussions often get out of hand. But sometimes there is no escaping ...

So here is some ammunition. The main advantages of LaTeX over normal word processors are the following:

- Professionally crafted layouts are available, which make a document really look as if "printed."

- The typesetting of mathematical formulae is supported in a convenient way.

- Users only need to learn a few easy-to-understand commands that specify the logical structure of a document. They almost never need to tinker with the actual layout of the document.

- Even complex structures such as footnotes, references, table of contents, and bibliographies can be generated easily.

- Free add-on packages exist for many typographical tasks not directly supported by basic LaTeX. For example, packages are available to include POSTSCRIPT graphics or to typeset bibliographies conforming to exact standards. Many of these add-on packages are described in *The LaTeX Companion* [3].

- LaTeX encourages authors to write well-structured texts, because this is how LaTeX works—by specifying structure.

- TEX, the formatting engine of LATEX 2_ε, is highly portable and free. Therefore the system runs on almost any hardware platform available.

LATEX also has some disadvantages, and I guess it's a bit difficult for me to find any sensible ones, though I am sure other people can tell you hundreds ;-)

- LATEX does not work well for people who have sold their souls . . .

- Although some parameters can be adjusted within a predefined document layout, the design of a whole new layout is difficult and takes a lot of time.[3]

- It is very hard to write unstructured and disorganized documents.

- Your hamster might, despite some encouraging first steps, never be able to fully grasp the concept of Logical Markup.

1.3　LATEX Input Files

The input for LATEX is a plain text file. On Unix/Linux text files are pretty common. On windows, one would use Notepad to create a text file. It contains the text of the document, as well as the commands that tell LATEX how to typeset the text. If you are working with a LATEX IDE, it will contain a program for creating LATEX input files in text format.

1.3.1　Spaces

"Whitespace" characters, such as blank or tab, are treated uniformly as "space" by LATEX. *Several consecutive* whitespace characters are treated as *one* "space." Whitespace at the start of a line is generally ignored, and a single line break is treated as "whitespace."

An empty line between two lines of text defines the end of a paragraph. *Several* empty lines are treated the same as *one* empty line. The text below is an example. On the left hand side is the text from the input file, and on the right hand side is the formatted output.

```
It does not matter whether you
enter one or several     spaces
after a word.

An empty line starts a new
paragraph.
```

> It does not matter whether you enter one or several spaces after a word.
>
> An empty line starts a new paragraph.

---

[3]Rumour says that this is one of the key elements that will be addressed in the upcoming LATEX3 system.

1.3.2 Special Characters

The following symbols are reserved characters that either have a special
meaning under LATEX or are not available in all the fonts. If you enter them
directly in your text, they will normally not print, but rather coerce LATEX
to do things you did not intend.

>   # $ %   ^   &   _   {   }   ~   \

As you will see, these characters can be used in your documents all the
same by using a prefix backslash:

```
\# \$ \% \^{} \& \_ \{ \} \~{}
\textbackslash
```

> # $ % ^ & _ { } ~ \

The other symbols and many more can be printed with special commands
in mathematical formulae or as accents. The backslash character \ can *not*
be entered by adding another backslash in front of it (\\); this sequence is
used for line breaking. Use the `\textbackslash` command instead.

1.3.3 LATEX Commands

LATEX commands are case sensitive, and take one of the following two formats:

- They start with a backslash \ and then have a name consisting of
  letters only. Command names are terminated by a space, a number or
  any other 'non-letter.'

- They consist of a backslash and exactly one non-letter.

- Many commands exist in a 'starred variant' where a star is appended
  to the command name.

LATEX ignores whitespace after commands. If you want to get a space after
a command, you have to put either an empty parameter {} and a blank or a
special spacing command after the command name. The empty parameter
{} stops LATEX from eating up all the white space after the command name.

```
New \TeX users may miss whitespaces
after a command. % renders wrong
Experienced \TeX{} users are
\TeX perts, and know how to use
whitespaces. % renders correct
```

> New TEXusers may miss whitespaces af-
> ter a command. Experienced TEX users
> are TEXperts, and know how to use white-
> spaces.

Some commands require a parameter, which has to be given between
curly braces { } after the command name. Some commands take optional
parameters, which are inserted after the command name in square brackets [ ].

$$\backslash command\,[optional\ parameter]\,\{parameter\}$$

The next examples use some LaTeX commands. Don't worry about them; they will be explained later.

```
You can \textsl{lean} on me!
```

> You can *lean* on me!

```
Please, start a new line
right here!\newline
Thank you!
```

> Please, start a new line right here!
> Thank you!

1.3.4   Comments

When LaTeX encounters a % character while processing an input file, it ignores the rest of the present line, the line break, and all whitespace at the beginning of the next line.

This can be used to write notes into the input file, which will not show up in the printed version.

```
This is an % stupid
% Better: instructive <----
example: Supercal%
            ifragilist%
    icexpialidocious
```

> This is an example: Supercalifragilisticex-
> pialidocious

The % character can also be used to split long input lines where no whitespace or line breaks are allowed.

For longer comments you could use the `comment` environment provided by the `verbatim` package. Add the line `\usepackage{verbatim}` to the preamble of your document as explained below to use this command.

```
This is another
\begin{comment}
rather stupid,
but helpful
\end{comment}
example for embedding
comments in your document.
```

> This is another example for embedding
> comments in your document.

Note that this won't work inside complex environments, like math for example.

1.4 Input File Structure

When LaTeX 2$_\varepsilon$ processes an input file, it expects it to follow a certain structure. Thus every input file must start with the command

```
\documentclass{...}
```

This specifies what sort of document you intend to write. After that, add commands to influence the style of the whole document, or load packages that add new features to the LaTeX system. To load such a package you use the command

```
\usepackage{...}
```

When all the setup work is done,[4] you start the body of the text with the command

```
\begin{document}
```

Now you enter the text mixed with some useful LaTeX commands. At the end of the document you add the

```
\end{document}
```

command, which tells LaTeX to call it a day. Anything that follows this command will be ignored by LaTeX.

Figure 1.1 shows the contents of a minimal LaTeX 2$_\varepsilon$ file. A slightly more complicated input file is given in Figure 1.2.

1.5 A Typical Command Line Session

I bet you must be dying to try out the neat small LaTeX input file shown on page 7. Here is some help: LaTeX itself comes without a GUI or fancy buttons to press. It is just a program that crunches away at your input file. Some LaTeX installations feature a graphical front-end where there is a LaTeX button to start compiling your input file. On other systems there might be

---

[4]The area between `\documentclass` and `\begin{document}` is called the *preamble*.

```
\documentclass{article}
\begin{document}
Small is beautiful.
\end{document}
```

Figure 1.1: A Minimal LaTeX File.

some typing involved, so here is how to coax LaTeX into compiling your input file on a text based system. Please note: this description assumes that a working LaTeX installation already sits on your computer.[5]

1. Edit/Create your LaTeX input file. This file must be plain ASCII text. On Unix all the editors will create just that. On Windows you might want to make sure that you save the file in ASCII or *Plain Text* format. When picking a name for your file, make sure it bears the extension `.tex`.

2. Open a shell or cmd window, cd to the directory where your input file is located and run LaTeX on your input file. If successful you will end up with a `.dvi` file. It may be necessary to run LaTeX several times to get the table of contents and all internal references right. When your input file has a bug LaTeX will tell you about it and stop processing your input file. Type `ctrl-D` to get back to the command line.

```
latex foo.tex
```

3. Now you may view the DVI file. There are several ways to do that.

---

[5]This is the case with most well groomed Unix Systems, and ... Real Men use Unix, so ... ;-)

```
\documentclass[a4paper,11pt]{article}
% define the title
\author{H.~Partl}
\title{Minimalism}
\begin{document}
% generates the title
\maketitle
% insert the table of contents
\tableofcontents
\section{Some Interesting Words}
Well, and here begins my lovely article.
\section{Good Bye World}
\ldots{} and here it ends.
\end{document}
```

Figure 1.2: Example of a Realistic Journal Article. Note that all the commands you see in this example will be explained later in the introduction.

Look at the file on screen with

```
xdvi foo.dvi &
```

This only works on Unix with X11. If you are on Windows you might want to try `yap` (yet another previewer).

Convert the dvi file to POSTSCRIPT for printing or viewing with GhostScript.

```
dvips -Pcmz foo.dvi -o foo.ps
```

If you are lucky your LaTeX system even comes with the `dvipdf` tool, which allows you to convert your `.dvi` files straight into pdf.

```
dvipdf foo.dvi
```

1.6 The Layout of the Document

1.6.1 Document Classes

The first information LaTeX needs to know when processing an input file is the type of document the author wants to create. This is specified with the `\documentclass` command.

```
\documentclass[options]{class}
```

Here *class* specifies the type of document to be created. Table 1.1 lists the document classes explained in this introduction. The LaTeX 2_ε distribution provides additional classes for other documents, including letters and slides. The *options* parameter customises the behaviour of the document class. The options have to be separated by commas. The most common options for the standard document classes are listed in Table 1.2.

Example: An input file for a LaTeX document could start with the line

```
\documentclass[11pt,twoside,a4paper]{article}
```

which instructs LaTeX to typeset the document as an *article* with a base font size of *eleven points*, and to produce a layout suitable for *double sided* printing on *A4 paper*.

1.6.2   Packages

While writing your document, you will probably find that there are some areas where basic LaTeX cannot solve your problem. If you want to include graphics, coloured text or source code from a file into your document, you need to enhance the capabilities of LaTeX. Such enhancements are called packages. Packages are activated with the

```
\usepackage[options]{package}
```

command, where *package* is the name of the package and *options* is a list of keywords that trigger special features in the package. The `\usepackage` command goes into the preamble of the document. See section 1.4 for details.

Some packages come with the LaTeX 2_ε base distribution (See Table 1.3). Others are provided separately. You may find more information on the packages installed at your site in your *Local Guide* [5]. The prime source for information about LaTeX packages is *The LaTeX Companion* [3]. It contains descriptions on hundreds of packages, along with information of how to write your own extensions to LaTeX 2_ε.

Modern TeX distributions come with a large number of packages preinstalled. If you are working on a Unix system, use the command `texdoc` for accessing package documentation.

Table 1.1: Document Classes.

`article` for articles in scientific journals, presentations, short reports, program documentation, invitations, ...

`proc` a class for proceedings based on the article class.

`minimal` is as small as it can get. It only sets a page size and a base font. It is mainly used for debugging purposes.

`report` for longer reports containing several chapters, small books, PhD theses, ...

`book` for real books

`slides` for slides. The class uses big sans serif letters. You might want to consider using the Beamer class instead.

Table 1.2: Document Class Options.

`10pt, 11pt, 12pt`   Sets the size of the main font in the document. If no option is specified, `10pt` is assumed.

`a4paper, letterpaper, ...`   Defines the paper size. The default size is `letterpaper`. Besides that, `a5paper`, `b5paper`, `executivepaper`, and `legalpaper` can be specified.

`fleqn`   Typesets displayed formulae left-aligned instead of centred.

`leqno`   Places the numbering of formulae on the left hand side instead of the right.

`titlepage, notitlepage`   Specifies whether a new page should be started after the document title or not. The `article` class does not start a new page by default, while `report` and `book` do.

`onecolumn, twocolumn`   Instructs LaTeX to typeset the document in one column or two columns.

`twoside, oneside`   Specifies whether double or single sided output should be generated. The classes `article` and `report` are single sided and the `book` class is double sided by default. Note that this option concerns the style of the document only. The option `twoside` does *not* tell the printer you use that it should actually make a two-sided printout.

`landscape`   Changes the layout of the document to print in landscape mode.

`openright, openany`   Makes chapters begin either only on right hand pages or on the next page available. This does not work with the `article` class, as it does not know about chapters. The `report` class by default starts chapters on the next page available and the `book` class starts them on right hand pages.

Table 1.3: Some of the Packages Distributed with LaTeX.

---

doc Allows the documentation of LaTeX programs.
Described in `doc.dtx`[a] and in *The LaTeX Companion* [3].

exscale Provides scaled versions of the math extension font.
Described in `ltexscale.dtx`.

fontenc Specifies which font encoding LaTeX should use.
Described in `ltoutenc.dtx`.

ifthen Provides commands of the form
'if... then do... otherwise do....'
Described in `ifthen.dtx` and *The LaTeX Companion* [3].

latexsym To access the LaTeX symbol font, you should use the `latexsym` package. Described in `latexsym.dtx` and in *The LaTeX Companion* [3].

makeidx Provides commands for producing indexes. Described in section 4.3 and in *The LaTeX Companion* [3].

syntonly Processes a document without typesetting it.

inputenc Allows the specification of an input encoding such as ASCII, ISO Latin-1, ISO Latin-2, 437/850 IBM code pages, Apple Macintosh, Next, ANSI-Windows or user-defined one. Described in `inputenc.dtx`.

---

[a]This file should be installed on your system, and you should be able to get a `dvi` file by typing `latex doc.dtx` in any directory where you have write permission. The same is true for all the other files mentioned in this table.

1.6.3 Page Styles

LaTeX supports three predefined header/footer combinations—so-called page styles. The *style* parameter of the

> `\pagestyle{`*style*`}`

command defines which one to use. Table 1.4 lists the predefined page styles.

Table 1.4: The Predefined Page Styles of LaTeX.

plain prints the page numbers on the bottom of the page, in the middle of the footer. This is the default page style.

headings prints the current chapter heading and the page number in the header on each page, while the footer remains empty. (This is the style used in this document)

empty sets both the header and the footer to be empty.

It is possible to change the page style of the current page with the command

> `\thispagestyle{`*style*`}`

A description how to create your own headers and footers can be found in *The LaTeX Companion* [3] and in section 4.4 on page 87.

1.7 Files You Might Encounter

When you work with LaTeX you will soon find yourself in a maze of files with various extensions and probably no clue. The following list explains the various file types you might encounter when working with TeX. Please note that this table does not claim to be a complete list of extensions, but if you find one missing that you think is important, please drop me a line.

.tex LaTeX or TeX input file. Can be compiled with `latex`.

.sty LaTeX Macro package. Load this into your LaTeX document using the `\usepackage` command.

.dtx Documented TeX. This is the main distribution format for LaTeX style files. If you process a .dtx file you get documented macro code of the LaTeX package contained in the .dtx file.

.ins The installer for the files contained in the matching .dtx file. If you download a LATEX package from the net, you will normally get a .dtx and a .ins file. Run LATEX on the .ins file to unpack the .dtx file.

.cls Class files define what your document looks like. They are selected with the \documentclass command.

.fd Font description file telling LATEX about new fonts.

The following files are generated when you run LATEX on your input file:

.dvi Device Independent File. This is the main result of a LATEX compile run. Look at its content with a DVI previewer program or send it to a printer with **dvips** or a similar application.

.log Gives a detailed account of what happened during the last compiler run.

.toc Stores all your section headers. It gets read in for the next compiler run and is used to produce the table of contents.

.lof This is like .toc but for the list of figures.

.lot And again the same for the list of tables.

.aux Another file that transports information from one compiler run to the next. Among other things, the .aux file is used to store information associated with cross-references.

.idx If your document contains an index. LATEX stores all the words that go into the index in this file. Process this file with **makeindex**. Refer to section 4.3 on page 86 for more information on indexing.

.ind The processed .idx file, ready for inclusion into your document on the next compile cycle.

.ilg Logfile telling what **makeindex** did.

1.8 Big Projects

When working on big documents, you might want to split the input file into several parts. LATEX has two commands that help you to do that.

```
\include{filename}
```

Use this command in the document body to insert the contents of another file named *filename.tex*. Note that LATEX will start a new page before processing the material input from *filename.tex*.

The second command can be used in the preamble. It allows you to instruct LaTeX to only input some of the \included files.

> \includeonly{*filename*,*filename*,...}

After this command is executed in the preamble of the document, only \include commands for the filenames that are listed in the argument of the \includeonly command will be executed.

The \include command starts typesetting the included text on a new page. This is helpful when you use \includeonly, because the page breaks will not move, even when some include files are omitted. Sometimes this might not be desirable. In this case, use the

> \input{*filename*}

command. It simply includes the file specified. No flashy suits, no strings attached.

To make LaTeX quickly check your document use the **syntonly** package. This makes LaTeX skim through your document only checking for proper syntax and usage of the commands, but doesn't produce any (DVI) output. As LaTeX runs faster in this mode you may save yourself valuable time. Usage is very simple:

```
\usepackage{syntonly}
\syntaxonly
```

When you want to produce pages, just comment out the second line (by adding a percent sign).

Chapter 2

Typesetting Text

After reading the previous chapter, you should know about the basic stuff of which a LaTeX 2$_\varepsilon$ document is made. In this chapter I will fill in the remaining structure you will need to know in order to produce real world material.

2.1 The Structure of Text and Language

By Hanspeter Schmid <hanspi@schmid-werren.ch>

The main point of writing a text (some modern DAAC[1] literature excluded), is to convey ideas, information, or knowledge to the reader. The reader will understand the text better if these ideas are well-structured, and will see and feel this structure much better if the typographical form reflects the logical and semantical structure of the content.

LaTeX is different from other typesetting systems in that you just have to tell it the logical and semantical structure of a text. It then derives the typographical form of the text according to the "rules" given in the document class file and in various style files.

The most important text unit in LaTeX (and in typography) is the paragraph. We call it "text unit" because a paragraph is the typographical form that should reflect one coherent thought, or one idea. You will learn in the following sections how to force line breaks with e.g. \\, and paragraph breaks with e.g. leaving an empty line in the source code. Therefore, if a new thought begins, a new paragraph should begin, and if not, only line breaks should be used. If in doubt about paragraph breaks, think about your text as a conveyor of ideas and thoughts. If you have a paragraph break, but the old thought continues, it should be removed. If some totally new line of thought occurs in the same paragraph, then it should be broken.

Most people completely underestimate the importance of well-placed paragraph breaks. Many people do not even know what the meaning of

---

[1] Different At All Cost, a translation of the Swiss German UVA (Um's Verrecken Anders).

a paragraph break is, or, especially in LaTeX, introduce paragraph breaks without knowing it. The latter mistake is especially easy to make if equations are used in the text. Look at the following examples, and figure out why sometimes empty lines (paragraph breaks) are used before and after the equation, and sometimes not. (If you don't yet understand all commands well enough to understand these examples, please read this and the following chapter, and then read this section again.)

```
% Example 1
\ldots when Einstein introduced his formula
\begin{equation}
  e = m \cdot c^2 \; ,
\end{equation}
which is at the same time the most widely known
and the least well understood physical formula.


% Example 2
\ldots from which follows Kirchhoff's current law:
\begin{equation}
  \sum_{k=1}^{n} I_k = 0 \; .
\end{equation}

Kirchhoff's voltage law can be derived \ldots


% Example 3
\ldots which has several advantages.

\begin{equation}
  I_D = I_F - I_R
\end{equation}
is the core of a very different transistor model. \ldots
```

The next smaller text unit is a sentence. In English texts, there is a larger space after a period that ends a sentence than after one that ends an abbreviation. LaTeX tries to figure out which one you wanted to have. If LaTeX gets it wrong, you must tell it what you want. This is explained later in this chapter.

The structuring of text even extends to parts of sentences. Most languages have very complicated punctuation rules, but in many languages (including German and English), you will get almost every comma right if you remember what it represents: a short stop in the flow of language. If you are not sure about where to put a comma, read the sentence aloud and take a short breath at every comma. If this feels awkward at some place, delete that comma; if you feel the urge to breathe (or make a short stop) at some other place, insert a comma.

Finally, the paragraphs of a text should also be structured logically at a higher level, by putting them into chapters, sections, subsections, and so on. However, the typographical effect of writing e.g. \section{The Structure of Text and Language} is so obvious that it is almost self-evident how these high-level structures should be used.

2.2 Line Breaking and Page Breaking

2.2.1 Justified Paragraphs

Books are often typeset with each line having the same length. LaTeX inserts the necessary line breaks and spaces between words by optimizing the contents of a whole paragraph. If necessary, it also hyphenates words that would not fit comfortably on a line. How the paragraphs are typeset depends on the document class. Normally the first line of a paragraph is indented, and there is no additional space between two paragraphs. Refer to section 6.3.2 for more information.

In special cases it might be necessary to order LaTeX to break a line:

> \\ or \newline

starts a new line without starting a new paragraph.

> *

additionally prohibits a page break after the forced line break.

> \newpage

starts a new page.

> \linebreak[n], \nolinebreak[n], \pagebreak[n], \nopagebreak[n]

suggest places where a break may (or may not) happen. They enable the author to influence their actions with the optional argument n, which can be set to a number between zero and four. By setting n to a value below 4, you leave LaTeX the option of ignoring your command if the result would look very bad. Do not confuse these "break" commands with the "new" commands. Even when you give a "break" command, LaTeX still tries to even out the right border of the line and the total length of the page, as described in the next section; this can lead to unpleasant gaps in your text. If you really want to start a "new line" or a "new page", then use the corresponding command. Guess their names!

LaTeX always tries to produce the best line breaks possible. If it cannot find a way to break the lines in a manner that meets its high standards, it lets one line stick out on the right of the paragraph. LaTeX then complains ("overfull hbox") while processing the input file. This happens most often when LaTeX cannot find a suitable place to hyphenate a word.[2] Instruct LaTeX to lower its standards a little by giving the `\sloppy` command. It prevents such over-long lines by increasing the inter-word spacing—even if the final output is not optimal. In this case a warning ("underfull hbox") is given to the user. In most such cases the result doesn't look very good. The command `\fussy` brings LaTeX back to its default behaviour.

2.2.2   Hyphenation

LaTeX hyphenates words whenever necessary. If the hyphenation algorithm does not find the correct hyphenation points, remedy the situation by using the following commands to tell TeX about the exception.

The command

```
\hyphenation{word list}
```

causes the words listed in the argument to be hyphenated only at the points marked by "-". The argument of the command should only contain words built from normal letters, or rather signs that are considered to be normal letters by LaTeX. The hyphenation hints are stored for the language that is active when the hyphenation command occurs. This means that if you place a hyphenation command into the preamble of your document it will influence the English language hyphenation. If you place the command after the `\begin{document}` and you are using some package for national language support like babel, then the hyphenation hints will be active in the language activated through babel.

The example below will allow "hyphenation" to be hyphenated as well as "Hyphenation", and it prevents "FORTRAN", "Fortran" and "fortran" from being hyphenated at all. No special characters or symbols are allowed in the argument.

Example:

```
\hyphenation{FORTRAN Hy-phen-a-tion}
```

---

[2] Although LaTeX gives you a warning when that happens (`Overfull \hbox`) and displays the offending line, such lines are not always easy to find. If you use the option `draft` in the `\documentclass` command, these lines will be marked with a thick black line on the right margin.

The command \- inserts a discretionary hyphen into a word. This also becomes the only point hyphenation is allowed in this word. This command is especially useful for words containing special characters (e.g. accented characters), because LaTeX does not automatically hyphenate words containing special characters.

```
I think this is: su\-per\-cal\-%
i\-frag\-i\-lis\-tic\-ex\-pi\-%
al\-i\-do\-cious
```

I think this is: supercalifragilisticexpiali-docious

Several words can be kept together on one line with the command

\mbox{*text*}

It causes its argument to be kept together under all circumstances.

```
My phone number will change soon.
It will be \mbox{0116 291 2319}.

The parameter
\mbox{\emph{filename}} should
contain the name of the file.
```

My phone number will change soon. It will be 0116 291 2319.
The parameter *filename* should contain the name of the file.

\fbox is similar to \mbox, but in addition there will be a visible box drawn around the content.

2.3 Ready-Made Strings

In some of the examples on the previous pages, you have seen some very simple LaTeX commands for typesetting special text strings:

Command	Example	Description
\today	July 18, 2015	Current date
\TeX	TeX	Your favorite typesetter
\LaTeX	LaTeX	The Name of the Game
\LaTeXe	LaTeX 2_ε	The current incarnation

2.4 Special Characters and Symbols

2.4.1 Quotation Marks

You should *not* use the " for quotation marks as you would on a typewriter. In publishing there are special opening and closing quotation marks. In LaTeX, use two ` (grave accent) for opening quotation marks and two ' (vertical quote) for closing quotation marks. For single quotes you use just one of each.

```
''Please press the 'x' key.''
```
"Please press the 'x' key."

Yes I know the rendering is not ideal, it's really a back-tick or grave accent (`) for opening quotes and vertical quote (') for closing, despite what the font chosen might suggest.

2.4.2   Dashes and Hyphens

LaTeX knows four kinds of dashes. Access three of them with different number of consecutive dashes. The fourth sign is actually not a dash at all—it is the mathematical minus sign:

```
daughter-in-law, X-rated\\
pages 13--67\\
yes---or no? \\
$0$, $1$ and $-1$
```
daughter-in-law, X-rated
pages 13–67
yes—or no?
0, 1 and -1

The names for these dashes are: '-' hyphen, '–' en-dash, '—' em-dash and '$-$' minus sign.

2.4.3   Tilde ($\sim$)

A character often seen in web addresses is the tilde. To generate this in LaTeX use \~{} but the result (˜) is not really what you want. Try this instead:

```
http://www.rich.edu/\~{}bush \\
http://www.clever.edu/$\sim$demo
```
http://www.rich.edu/˜bush
http://www.clever.edu/$\sim$demo

2.4.4   Slash (/)

In order to typeset a slash between two words, one can simply type e.g. `read/write`, but this makes LaTeX treat the two words as one. Hyphenation is disabled for these two words, so there may be 'overfull' errors. To overcome this, use \slash. For example type 'read\slash write' which allows hyphenation. But normal '/' character may be still used for ratios or units, e.g. `5 MB/s`.

2.4.5   Degree Symbol (∘)

Printing the degree symbol in pure LaTeX.

```
It's $-30\,^{\circ}\mathrm{C}$.
I will soon start to
super-conduct.
```

It's $-30\,^{\circ}$C. I will soon start to super-conduct.

The textcomp package makes the degree symbol also available as \textdegree or in combination with the C by using the \textcelsius.

```
30 \textcelsius{} is
86 \textdegree{}F.
```

30 °C is 86 °F.

2.4.6 The Euro Currency Symbol (€)

When writing about money these days, you need the Euro symbol. Many current fonts contain a Euro symbol. After loading the textcomp package in the preamble of your document

```
\usepackage{textcomp}
```

use the command

```
\texteuro
```

to access it.

If your font does not provide its own Euro symbol or if you do not like the font's Euro symbol, you have two more choices:

First the eurosym package. It provides the official Euro symbol:

```
\usepackage[official]{eurosym}
```

If you prefer a Euro symbol that matches your font, use the option gen in place of the official option.

Table 2.1: A bag full of Euro symbols

LM+textcomp	\texteuro	€	€	€
eurosym	\euro	€	€	€
[gen]eurosym	\euro	€	€	€

2.4.7   Ellipsis (...)

On a typewriter, a comma or a period takes the same amount of space as
any other letter. In book printing, these characters occupy only a little space
and are set very close to the preceding letter. Therefore, entering 'ellipsis'
by just typing three dots would produce the wrong result. Instead, there is
a special command for these dots. It is called

> `\ldots` (low dots)

`Not like this ... but like this:\\` `New York, Tokyo, Budapest, \ldots`	Not like this ... but like this: New York, Tokyo, Budapest, ...

2.4.8   Ligatures

Some letter combinations are typeset not just by setting the different letters
one after the other, but by actually using special symbols.

> ff fi fl ffi...   instead of   ff fi fl ffi ...

These so-called ligatures can be prohibited by inserting an `\mbox{}` between
the two letters in question. This might be necessary with words built from
two words.

`\Large Not shelfful\\` `but shelf\mbox{}ful`	Not shelfful but shelfful

2.4.9   Accents and Special Characters

LaTeX supports the use of accents and special characters from many languages.
Table 2.2 shows all sorts of accents being applied to the letter o. Naturally
other letters work too.

To place an accent on top of an i or a j, its dots have to be removed.
This is accomplished by typing `\i` and `\j`.

`H\^otel, na\"\i ve, \'el\`eve,\\` `sm\o rrebr\o d, !`Se\~norita!,\\` `Sch\"onbrunner Schlo\ss{}` `Stra\ss e`	Hôtel, naïve, élève, smørrebrød, ¡Señorita!, Schönbrunner Schloß Straße

2.5 International Language Support

When you write documents in languages other than English, there are three areas where LaTeX has to be configured appropriately:

1. All automatically generated text strings[3] have to be adapted to the new language. For many languages, these changes can be accomplished by using the babel package by Johannes Braams.

2. LaTeX needs to know the hyphenation rules for the new language. Getting hyphenation rules into LaTeX is a bit more tricky. It means rebuilding the format file with different hyphenation patterns enabled. Your *Local Guide* [5] should give more information on this.

3. Language specific typographic rules. In French for example, there is a mandatory space before each colon character (:).

If your system is already configured appropriately, activate the babel package by adding the command

```
\usepackage[language]{babel}
```

after the \documentclass command. A list of the *language*s built into your LaTeX system will be displayed every time the compiler is started. Babel will automatically activate the appropriate hyphenation rules for the language you choose. If your LaTeX format does not support hyphenation in the language of your choice, babel will still work but will disable hyphenation, which has quite a negative effect on the appearance of the typeset document.

---

[3]Table of Contents, List of Figures, . . .

Table 2.2: Accents and Special Characters.

ò	\`o	ó	\'o	ô	\^o	õ	\~o
ō	\=o	ȯ	\.o	ö	\"o	ç	\c c
ŏ	\u o	ǒ	\v o	ő	\H o	ǫ	\c o
ọ	\d o	o̲	\b o	o͡o	\t oo		
œ	\oe	Œ	\OE	æ	\ae	Æ	\AE
å	\aa	Å	\AA				
ø	\o	Ø	\O	ł	\l	Ł	\L
ı	\i	J	\j	¡	!\`	¿	?\`

Babel also specifies new commands for some languages, which simplify the input of special characters. The German language, for example, contains a lot of umlauts (äöü). With babel loaded, enter an ö by typing "o instead of \"o.

If you call babel with multiple languages

```
\usepackage[languageA,languageB]{babel}
```

then the last language in the option list will be active (i.e. languageB). Use the command

```
\selectlanguage{languageA}
```

to change the active language.

Most modern computer systems allow you to input letters of national alphabets directly from the keyboard. In order to handle a variety of input encodings used for different groups of languages and/or on different computer platforms LaTeX employs the inputenc package:

```
\usepackage[encoding]{inputenc}
```

When using this package, you should consider that other people might not be able to display your input files on their computer, because they use a different encoding. For example, the German umlaut ä on OS/2 is encoded as 132, on Unix systems using ISO-LATIN 1 it is encoded as 228, while in Cyrillic encoding cp1251 for Windows this letter does not exist at all; therefore you should use this feature with care. The following encodings may come in handy, depending on the type of system you are working on[4]

Operating	encodings	
system	western Latin	Cyrillic
Mac	applemac	macukr
Unix	latin1	koi8-ru
Windows	ansinew	cp1251
DOS, OS/2	cp850	cp866nav

```
\usepackage[utf8]{inputenc}
```

will enable you to create LaTeX input files in utf8, a multi-byte encoding in which each character can be encoded in as little as one byte and as many as four bytes.

---

[4]To learn more about supported input encodings for Latin-based and Cyrillic-based languages, read the documentation for inputenc.dtx and cyinpenc.dtx respectively. Section 4.6 tells how to produce package documentation.

Since the turn of the Century most Operating Systems are based on Unicode (Windows XP, MacOS X). Therefore it is recommended to use `utf8` for any new project. The `utf8` encoding used by inputenc only defines the characters that are actually provided by the fonts used. If you need more (non-latin) characters have a look at X̄ǝLATEX in section 4.8 a Unicode based TEX-engine.

Font encoding is a different matter. It defines at which position inside a TEX-font each letter is stored. Multiple input encodings could be mapped into one font encoding, which reduces the number of required font sets. Font encodings are handled through fontenc package:

```
\usepackage[encoding]{fontenc}
```

where *encoding* is font encoding. It is possible to load several encodings simultaneously.

The default LATEX font encoding is `OT1`, the encoding of the original Computer Modern TEX font. It contains only the 128 characters of the 7-bit ASCII character set. When accented characters are required, TEX creates them by combining a normal character with an accent. While the resulting output looks perfect, this approach stops the automatic hyphenation from working inside words containing accented characters. Besides, some Latin letters could not be created by combining a normal character with an accent, to say nothing about letters of non-Latin alphabets, such as Greek or Cyrillic.

To overcome these shortcomings, several 8-bit CM-like font sets were created. *Extended Cork* (EC) fonts in `T1` encoding contains letters and punctuation characters for most of the European languages using Latin script. The LH font set contains letters necessary to typeset documents in languages using Cyrillic script. Because of the large number of Cyrillic glyphs, they are arranged into four font encodings—`T2A`, `T2B`, `T2C`, and `X2`.[5] The CB bundle contains fonts in `LGR` encoding for the composition of Greek text.

Improve/enable hyphenation in non-English documents by using these fonts. Another advantage of using new CM-like fonts is that they provide fonts of CM families in all weights, shapes, and optically scaled font sizes.

2.5.1 Support for Portuguese

By Demerson Andre Polli <polli@linux.ime.usp.br>

To enable hyphenation and change all automatic text to Portuguese, use the

---

[5]Find a list of languages supported by each of these encodings in [11].

Table 2.3: Preamble for Portuguese documents.

```
\usepackage[portuguese]{babel}
\usepackage[latin1]{inputenc}
\usepackage[T1]{fontenc}
```

command:

```
\usepackage[portuguese]{babel}
```

Or if you are in Brazil, substitute `brazilian` as the language.
As there are a lot of accents in Portuguese you might want to use

```
\usepackage[latin1]{inputenc}
```

to be able to input them correctly as well as

```
\usepackage[T1]{fontenc}
```

to get the hyphenation right.

See table 2.3 for the preamble you need to write in the Portuguese language. Note that the example is for the latin1 input encoding. Modern systems might be using utf8 instead.

2.5.2 Support for French

By Daniel Flipo <daniel.flipo@univ-lille1.fr>

Some hints for those creating French documents with LaTeX: load French language support with the following command:

```
\usepackage[francais]{babel}
```

This enables French hyphenation, if you have configured your LaTeX system accordingly. It also changes all automatic text into French: \chapter prints Chapitre, \today prints the current date in French and so on. A set of new commands also becomes available, which allows you to write French input files more easily. Check out table 2.4 for inspiration.

You will also notice that the layout of lists changes when switching to the French language. For more information on what the `francais` option of `babel` does and how to customize its behaviour, run LaTeX on file `frenchb.dtx` and read the produced file `frenchb.dvi`.

Table 2.4: Special commands for French.

`\og guillemets \fg{}`	« guillemets »
`M\up{me}, D\up{r}`	Mme, D^{r}
`1\ier{}, 1\iere{}, 1\ieres{}`	1er, 1re, 1res
`2\ieme{} 4\iemes{}`	2^{e} 4^{es}
`\No 1, \no 2`	N° 1, n° 2
`20~\degres C, 45\degres`	20 °C, 45°
`\bsc{M. Durand}`	M. Durand
`\nombre{1234,56789}`	1 234,567 89

Recent versions of frenchb rely on numprint to implement the `\nombre` command.

2.5.3 Support for German

Some hints for those creating German documents with LaTeX: load German language support with the following command:

```
\usepackage[german]{babel}
```

This enables German hyphenation, if you have configured your LaTeX system accordingly. It also changes all automatic text into German. Eg. "Chapter" becomes "Kapitel." A set of new commands also becomes available, which allows you to write German input files more quickly even when you don't use the inputenc package. Check out table 2.5 for inspiration. With inputenc, all this becomes moot, but your text also is locked in a particular encoding world.

In German books you often find French quotation marks («guillemets»). German typesetters, however, use them differently. A quote in a German book would look like »this«. In the German speaking part of Switzerland, typesetters use «guillemets» the same way the French do.

A major problem arises from the use of commands like `\flq`: If you use the OT1 font (which is the default font) the guillemets will look like the math symbol "$\ll$", which turns a typesetter's stomach. T1 encoded fonts, on the other hand, do contain the required symbols. So if you are using this type of quote, make sure you use the T1 encoding. (`\usepackage[T1]{fontenc}`)

Table 2.5: German Special Characters.

"a	ä	"s	ß
"`		"'	"
	„		
"< or \flqq	«	"> or \frqq	»
\flq	‹	\frq	›
\dq	"		

2.5.4　Support for Korean[6]

To process Hangul[7] characters or prepare a document written in Korean using LaTeX, put the following code in the preamble of the document.

```
\usepackage{kotex}
```

A document containing the declaration above will have to be processed by pdfLaTeX, XƎLaTeX, or LuaLaTeX. Make sure that the input file written in Hangul is encoded in Unicode UTF-8. The package called ko.TeX[8] is under continuous development by the Korean TeX Users Group[9] and the Korean TeX Society.[10] Many people use this package to create Korean documents for their everyday needs. ko.TeX has been available on CTAN since 2014. It is included TeX Live, MiKTeX and other modern TeX distributions. So in all likelyhood you can start working right away without installing any extra packages.

ko.TeX does not use the `babel` package. Many functions related to Korean can be activated using the options and configuration commands provided by the kotex package. If you want to compose a real world Korean document, you are advised to consult the package documentation (These documents are written in Korean).

With ko.TeX, you also get **oblivoir**, a **memoir**-based document class, tailored for Korean document preparation. So your Korean document would

---

[6]Written by Karnes Kim <karnes@ktug.org> and Kihwang Lee <leekh@ktug.org> on behalf of the Korean TeX Users Group and the Korean TeX Society.

[7]Hangul is the name of the Korean writing system. Refer to http://en.wikipedia.org/wiki/Hangul for more information.

[8]Reads "Korean TeX". ko.TeX is the name of a collection of packages including `cjk-ko`, `kotex-utf`, `xetexko`, and `luatexko`.

[9]http://ktug.org

[10]http://ktug.kr

Table 2.6: Preamble for Greek documents.

```
\usepackage[english,greek]{babel}
\usepackage[iso-8859-7]{inputenc}
```

start like this:

```
\documentclass{oblivoir}
```

To generate an index for a Korean document, execute `komkindex` instead of `makeindex`. It is a version of the `makeindex` utility modified for Korean processing. For lexicographical sorting of the Korean index items, you can use index style `kotex.ist` provided by ko.TEX as follows:

```
komkindex -s kotex foo.idx
```

You can also use `xindy` for index generation as the Korean module for `xindy` is included in TEX Live.

There is another Korean/Hangul typesetting package called CJK. As the name of the package suggests, it has facilities for typesetting Chinese, Japanese, and Korean characters. It supports multiple encodings of the CJK characters. The following is a simple example of typesetting UTF-8 encoded Hangul using CJK package. It is useful when you submit a manuscript to some academic journals that allow typesetting author names in native languages.

```
\usepackage{CJK}

\begin{CJK}{UTF8}{}
\CJKfamily{nanummj}
...
\end{CJK}
```

2.5.5 Writing in Greek

By Nikolaos Pothitos <pothitos@di.uoa.gr>

See table 2.6 for the preamble you need to write in the Greek language. This preamble enables hyphenation and changes all automatic text to Greek.[11]

---

[11] If you select the `utf8x` option for the package `inputenc`, LaTeX will understand Greek and polytonic Greek Unicode characters.

A set of new commands also becomes available, which allows you to write Greek input files more easily. In order to temporarily switch to English and vice versa, one can use the commands \textlatin{*english text*} and \textgreek{*greek text*} that both take one argument which is then typeset using the requested font encoding. Otherwise use the command \selectlanguage{...} described in a previous section. Check out table 2.7 for some Greek punctuation characters. Use \euro for the Euro symbol.

Table 2.7: Greek Special Characters.

;	·	?	;
((	«	))	»
‛ ‛	‛	,,	,

2.5.6 Support for Cyrillic

By Maksym Polyakov <polyama@myrealbox.com>

Version 3.7h of babel includes support for the T2* encodings and for typesetting Bulgarian, Russian and Ukrainian texts using Cyrillic letters.

Support for Cyrillic is based on standard LaTeX mechanisms plus the fontenc and inputenc packages. But, if you are going to use Cyrillics in math mode, you need to load mathtext package before fontenc:[12]

```
\usepackage{mathtext}
\usepackage[T1,T2A]{fontenc}
\usepackage[koi8-ru]{inputenc}
\usepackage[english,bulgarian,russian,ukranian]{babel}
```

Generally, babel will authomatically choose the default font encoding, for the above three languages this is T2A. However, documents are not restricted to a single font encoding. For multi-lingual documents using Cyrillic and Latin-based languages it makes sense to include Latin font encoding explicitly. babel will take care of switching to the appropriate font encoding when a different language is selected within the document.

In addition to enabling hyphenations, translating automatically generated text strings, and activating some language specific typographic rules (like \frenchspacing), babel provides some commands allowing typesetting according to the standards of Bulgarian, Russian, or Ukrainian languages.

For all three languages, language specific punctuation is provided: The Cyrillic dash for the text (it is little narrower than Latin dash and surrounded

---

[12]If you use $\mathcal{A}\mathcal{M}\mathcal{S}$-LaTeX packages, load them before fontenc and babel as well.

by tiny spaces), a dash for direct speech, quotes, and commands to facilitate hyphenation, see Table 2.8.

Table 2.8: The extra definitions made by Bulgarian, Russian, and Ukrainian options of babel

`"|`	disable ligature at this position.
`"-`	an explicit hyphen sign, allowing hyphenation in the rest of the word.
`"---`	Cyrillic emdash in plain text.
`"---~`	Cyrillic emdash in compound names (surnames).
`"--*`	Cyrillic emdash for denoting direct speech.
`""`	like `"-`, but producing no hyphen sign (for compound words with hyphen, e.g. `x-""y` or some other signs as "disable/enable").
`"~`	for a compound word mark without a breakpoint.
`"=`	for a compound word mark with a breakpoint, allowing hyphenation in the composing words.
`",`	thinspace for initials with a breakpoint in following surname.
`"'`	for German left double quotes (looks like „).
`"'`	for German right double quotes (looks like ").
`"<`	for French left double quotes (looks like ≪).
`">`	for French right double quotes (looks like ≫).

The Russian and Ukrainian options of babel define the commands `\Asbuk` and `\asbuk`, which act like `\Alph` and `\alph`[13], but produce capital and small letters of Russian or Ukrainian alphabets (whichever is the active language of the document). The Bulgarian option of babel provides the commands `\enumBul` and `\enumLat` (`\enumEng`), which make `\Alph` and `\alph` produce letters of either Bulgarian or Latin (English) alphabets. The default behaviour of `\Alph` and `\alph` for the Bulgarian language option is to produce letters from the Bulgarian alphabet.

2.5.7 Support for Mongolian

To use LaTeX for typesetting Mongolian you have a choice between two packages: Multilingual Babel and MonTeX by Oliver Corff.

MonTeX includes support for both Cyrillic and traditional Mongolian Script. In order to access the commands of MonTeX, add:

```
\usepackage[language,encoding]{mls}
```

to the preamble. Choose the *language* option xalx to generate captions and dates in Modern Mongolian. To write a complete document in the

---

[13]the commands for turning counters into a, b, c, . . .

traditional Mongolian script you have to choose bicig for the *language* option. The document language option bicig enables the "Simplified Transliteration" input method.

Enable and disable Latin Transliteration Mode with

```
\SetDocumentEncodingLMC
```

and

```
\SetDocumentEncodingNeutral
```

More information about MonTEX is available from `CTAN://language/mongolian/montex/doc`.

Mongolian Cyrillic script is supported by babel. Activate Mongolian language support with the following commands:

```
\usepackage[T2A]{fontenc}
\usepackage[mn]{inputenc}
\usepackage[mongolian]{babel}
```

where `mn` is the `cp1251` input encoding. For a more modern approach invoke `utf8` instead.

2.5.8 The Unicode option

By Axel Kielhorn <A.Kielhorn@web.de>

Unicode is the way to go if you want to include several languages in one document, especially when these languages are not using the latin script. There are two TEX-engines that are capable of processing Unicode input:

X_ETEX was developed for MacOS X but is now available for all architectures. It was first included into TexLive 2007.

LuaTEX is the successor of pdfTEX. It was first included into TexLive 2008.

The following describes X_ELATEX as distributed with TexLive 2010.

Quickstart

To convert an existing LATEX file to X_ELATEX the following needs to be done:

1. Save the file as UTF-8

2. Remove

```
\usepackage{inputenc}
\usepackage{fontenc}
\usepackage{textcomp}
```

from the preamble.

3. Change

```
\usepackage[languageA]{babel}
```

to

```
\usepackage{polyglossia}
\setdefaultlanguage[babelshorthands]{languageA}
```

4. Add

```
\usepackage[Ligatures=TeX]{fontspec}
```

to the preamble.

The package polyglossia[19] is a replacement for babel. It takes care of the hyphenation patterns and automatically generated text strings. The option `babelshorthands` enables babel compatible shorthands for german and catalan.

The package fontspec[21] handles font loading for XLATEX and LuaTEX. The default font is Latin Modern Roman. It is a little known fact that some TEX command are ligatures defined in the Computer Modern fonts. If you want to use them with a non-TEX font, you have to fake them. The option `Ligatures=TeX` defines the following ligatures:

--	–
---	—
''	"
``	"
!`	¡
?`	¿
,,	„
<<	«
>>	»

It's all Γρεεκ to me

So far there has been no advantage to using a Unicode TEX engine. This changes when we leave the Latin script and move to a more interesting language like Greek or Russian. With a Unicode based system, you can simply[14] enter the characters in your editor and TEX will understand them.

Writing in different languages is easy, just specify the languages in the preamble:

```
\setdefaultlanguage{english}
\setotherlanguage[babelshorthands]{german}
```

To write a paragraph in German, you can use the German environment:

```
English text.
\begin{german}
Deutscher Text.
\end{german}
More English text.
```

If you just need a word in a foreign language you can use the \text*language* command:

```
Englisch text. \textgerman{Gesundheit} is actually a German word.
```

This may look unnecessary since the only advantage is a correct hyphenation, but when the second language is a little bit more exotic it will be worth the effort.

Sometimes the font used in the main document does not contain glyphs that are required in the second language[15]. The solution is to define a font that will be used for that language. Whenever a new language is activated, **polyglossia** will first check whether a font has been defined for that language.

```
\newfontfamily\russianfont[Script=Cyrillic,(...)]{(font)}
```

Now you can write

```
\textrussian{Pravda} is a russian newspaper.
```

Since this document is written in Latin1-encoding, I cannot show the actual Cyrillic letters.

The package xgreek[22] offers support for writing either ancient or modern (monotonic or polytonic) greek.

---

[14]For small values of simple.

[15]Latin Modern does not contain Cyrillic letters

Right to Left (RTL) languages.

Some languages are written left to right, others are written right to left(RTL). polyglossia needs the bidi[23] package[16] in order to support RTL languages. The bidi package should be the last package you load, even after hyperref which is usually the last package. (Since polyglossia loads bidi this means that polyglossia should be the last package loaded.)

The package xepersian[24] offers support for the Persian language. It supplies Persian LaTeX-commands that allows you to enter commands like \section in Persian, which makes this really attractive to native speakers. xepersian is the only package that supports kashida with X∃LATEX. A package for Syriac which uses a similar algorithm is under development.

The IranNastaliq font provided by the SCICT[17] is available at their website http://www.scict.ir/Portal/Home/Default.aspx.

The arabxetex[20] package supports several languages with an Arabic script:

- arab (Arabic)

- persian

- urdu

- sindhi

- pashto

- ottoman (turk)

- kurdish

- kashmiri

- malay (jawi)

- uighur

It offers a font mapping that enables X∃LATEX to process input using the ArabTEX ASCII transcription.

Fonts that support several Arabic laguages are offered by the IRMUG[18] at http://wiki.irmug.org/index.php/X_Series_2.

There is no package available for Hebrew because none is needed. The Hebrew support in polyglossia should be sufficient. But you do need a suitable font with real Unicode Hebrew. SBL Hebrew is free for non-commercial use and available at http://www.sbl-site.org/educational/

---

[16]bidi does not support LuaTEX.
[17]Supreme Council of Information and Communication Technology
[18]Iranian Mac User Group

`biblicalfonts.aspx`. Another font available under the Open Font License
is Ezra SIL, available at `http://www.sil.org/computing/catalog/show_`
`software.asp?id=76`.

Remember to select the correct script:

```
\newfontfamily\hebrewfont[Script=Hebrew]{SBL Hebrew}
\newfontfamily\hebrewfont[Script=Hebrew]{Ezra SIL}
```

Chinese, Japanese and Korean (CJK)

The package xeCJK[25] takes care of font selection and punctuation for these
languages.

2.6   The Space Between Words

To get a straight right margin in the output, LaTeX inserts varying amounts
of space between the words. It inserts slightly more space at the end of a
sentence, as this makes the text more readable. LaTeX assumes that sentences
end with periods, question marks or exclamation marks. If a period follows
an uppercase letter, this is not taken as a sentence ending, since periods after
uppercase letters normally occur in abbreviations.

Any exception from these assumptions has to be specified by the author.
A backslash in front of a space generates a space that will not be enlarged. A
tilde '~' character generates a space that cannot be enlarged and additionally
prohibits a line break. The command `\@` in front of a period specifies that
this period terminates a sentence even when it follows an uppercase letter.

```
Mr.~Smith was happy to see her\\
cf.~Fig.~5\\
I like BASIC\@. What about you?
```
```
Mr. Smith was happy to see her
cf. Fig. 5
I like BASIC. What about you?
```

The additional space after periods can be disabled with the command

```
\frenchspacing
```

which tells LaTeX *not* to insert more space after a period than after an
ordinary character. This is very common in non-English languages, except
bibliographies. If you use `\frenchspacing`, the command `\@` is not necessary.

2.7   Titles, Chapters, and Sections

To help the reader find his or her way through your work, you should divide it into chapters, sections, and subsections. LaTeX supports this with special commands that take the section title as their argument. It is up to you to use them in the correct order.

The following sectioning commands are available for the `article` class:

```
\section{...}
\subsection{...}
\subsubsection{...}
\paragraph{...}
\subparagraph{...}
```

If you want to split your document into parts without influencing the section or chapter numbering use

```
\part{...}
```

When you work with the `report` or `book` class, an additional top-level sectioning command becomes available

```
\chapter{...}
```

As the `article` class does not know about chapters, it is quite easy to add articles as chapters to a book. The spacing between sections, the numbering and the font size of the titles will be set automatically by LaTeX.

Two of the sectioning commands are a bit special:

- The `\part` command does not influence the numbering sequence of chapters.

- The `\appendix` command does not take an argument. It just changes the chapter numbering to letters.[19]

LaTeX creates a table of contents by taking the section headings and page numbers from the last compile cycle of the document. The command

```
\tableofcontents
```

expands to a table of contents at the place it is issued. A new document has to be compiled ("LaTeXed") twice to get a correct table of contents. Sometimes it might be necessary to compile the document a third time. LaTeX will tell you when this is necessary.

---

[19]For the article style it changes the section numbering.

All sectioning commands listed above also exist as "starred" versions. A "starred" version of a command is built by adding a star * after the command name. This generates section headings that do not show up in the table of contents and are not numbered. The command `\section{Help}`, for example, would become `\section*{Help}`.

Normally the section headings show up in the table of contents exactly as they are entered in the text. Sometimes this is not possible, because the heading is too long to fit into the table of contents. The entry for the table of contents can then be specified as an optional argument in front of the actual heading.

```
\chapter[Title for the table of contents]{A long
        and especially boring title, shown in the text}
```

The title of the whole document is generated by issuing a

```
\maketitle
```

command. The contents of the title have to be defined by the commands

```
\title{...}, \author{...} and optionally \date{...}
```

before calling `\maketitle`. In the argument to `\author`, you can supply several names separated by `\and` commands.

An example of some of the commands mentioned above can be found in Figure 1.2 on page 8.

Apart from the sectioning commands explained above, LaTeX 2$_\varepsilon$ introduced three additional commands for use with the **book** class. They are useful for dividing your publication. The commands alter chapter headings and page numbering to work as you would expect in a book:

`\frontmatter` should be the very first command after the start of the document body (`\begin{document}`). It will switch page numbering to Roman numerals and sections will be non-enumerated as if you were using the starred sectioning commands (eg `\chapter*{Preface}`) but the sections will still show up in the table of contents.

`\mainmatter` comes right before the first chapter of the book. It turns on Arabic page numbering and restarts the page counter.

`\appendix` marks the start of additional material in your book. After this command chapters will be numbered with letters.

`\backmatter` should be inserted before the very last items in your book, such as the bibliography and the index. In the standard document classes, this has no visual effect.

2.8   Cross References

In books, reports and articles, there are often cross-references to figures, tables and special segments of text. LATEX provides the following commands for cross referencing

---

`\label{`*marker*`}`, `\ref{`*marker*`}` and `\pageref{`*marker*`}`

---

where *marker* is an identifier chosen by the user. LATEX replaces `\ref` by the number of the section, subsection, figure, table, or theorem after which the corresponding `\label` command was issued. `\pageref` prints the page number of the page where the `\label` command occurred.[20] As with section titles and page numbers for the table of contents, the numbers from the previous compile cycle are used.

```
A reference to this subsection
\label{sec:this} looks like:
''see section~\ref{sec:this} on
page~\pageref{sec:this}.''
```

A reference to this subsection looks like: "see section 2.8 on page 41."

2.9   Footnotes

With the command

`\footnote{`*footnote text*`}`

---

a footnote is printed at the foot of the current page. Footnotes should always be put[21] after the word or sentence they refer to. Footnotes referring to a sentence or part of it should therefore be put after the comma or period.[22]

```
Footnotes\footnote{This is
   a footnote.} are often used
by people using \LaTeX.
```

Footnotes[a] are often used by people using LATEX.

---
[a]This is a footnote.

---

[20]Note that these commands are not aware of what they refer to. `\label` just saves the last automatically generated number.

[21]"put" is one of the most common English words.

[22]Note that footnotes distract the reader from the main body of your document. After all, everybody reads the footnotes—we are a curious species, so why not just integrate everything you want to say into the body of the document?[23]

[23]A guidepost doesn't necessarily go where it's pointing to :-).

2.10   Emphasized Words

If a text is typed using a typewriter, important words are `emphasized` by
`underlining` them.

> `\underline{`*text*`}`

In printed books, however, words are emphasized by typesetting them in
an *italic* font. As an author you shouldn't care either way. The important
bit is, to tell LaTeX that a particular bit of text is important and should be
emphasized. Hence the command

> `\emph{`*text*`}`

to emphasize text. What the command actually does with its argument
depends on the context:

```
\emph{If you use
  emphasizing inside a piece
  of emphasized text, then
  \LaTeX{} uses the
  \emph{normal} font for
  emphasizing.}
```

> *If you use emphasizing inside a piece of
> emphasized text, then LaTeX uses the nor-
> mal font for emphasizing.*

If you want control over font and font size, section 6.2 on page 123 might
provide some inspiration.

2.11   Environments

> `\begin{`*environment*`}`   *text*   `\end{`*environment*`}`

Where *environment* is the name of the environment. Environments can be
nested within each other as long as the correct nesting order is maintained.

> `\begin{aaa}...\begin{bbb}...\end{bbb}...\end{aaa}`

In the following sections all important environments are explained.

2.11.1   Itemize, Enumerate, and Description

The `itemize` environment is suitable for simple lists, the `enumerate` environment for enumerated lists, and the `description` environment for descriptions.

```
\flushleft
\begin{enumerate}
\item You can nest the list
environments to your taste:
\begin{itemize}
\item But it might start to
look silly.
\item[-] With a dash.
\end{itemize}
\item Therefore remember:
\begin{description}
\item[Stupid] things will not
become smart because they are
in a list.
\item[Smart] things, though,
can be presented beautifully
in a list.
\end{description}
\end{enumerate}
```

> 1. You can nest the list environments to your taste:
>
>   • But it might start to look silly.
>   - With a dash.
>
> 2. Therefore remember:
>
>   **Stupid** things will not become smart because they are in a list.
>
>   **Smart** things, though, can be presented beautifully in a list.

2.11.2 Flushleft, Flushright, and Center

The environments `flushleft` and `flushright` generate paragraphs that are either left- or right-aligned. The `center` environment generates centred text. If you do not issue \\ to specify line breaks, LaTeX will automatically determine line breaks.

```
\begin{flushleft}
This text is\\ left-aligned.
\LaTeX{} is not trying to make
each line the same length.
\end{flushleft}
```

> This text is
> left-aligned. LaTeX is not trying to make each line the same length.

```
\begin{flushright}
This text is right-\\aligned.
\LaTeX{} is not trying to make
each line the same length.
\end{flushright}
```

> This text is right-aligned. LaTeX is not trying to make each line the same length.

```
\begin{center}
At the centre\\of the earth
\end{center}
```

> At the centre
> of the earth

2.11.3   Quote, Quotation, and Verse

The `quote` environment is useful for quotes, important phrases and examples.

```
A typographical rule of thumb
for the line length is:
\begin{quote}
On average, no line should
be longer than 66 characters.
\end{quote}
This is why \LaTeX{} pages have
such large borders by default
and also why multicolumn print
is used in newspapers.
```

> A typographical rule of thumb for the line length is:
>
> > On average, no line should be longer than 66 characters.
>
> This is why LaTeX pages have such large borders by default and also why multicolumn print is used in newspapers.

There are two similar environments: the `quotation` and the `verse` environments. The `quotation` environment is useful for longer quotes going over several paragraphs, because it indents the first line of each paragraph. The `verse` environment is useful for poems where the line breaks are important. The lines are separated by issuing a \\ at the end of a line and an empty line after each verse.

```
I know only one English poem by
heart. It is about Humpty Dumpty.
\begin{flushleft}
\begin{verse}
Humpty Dumpty sat on a wall:\\
Humpty Dumpty had a great fall.\\
All the King's horses and all
the King's men\\
Couldn't put Humpty together
again.
\end{verse}
\end{flushleft}
```

> I know only one English poem by heart. It is about Humpty Dumpty.
>
> > Humpty Dumpty sat on a
> > wall:
> > Humpty Dumpty had a great
> > fall.
> > All the King's horses and all
> > the King's men
> > Couldn't put Humpty
> > together again.

2.11.4   Abstract

In scientific publications it is customary to start with an abstract which gives the reader a quick overview of what to expect. LaTeX provides the `abstract` environment for this purpose. Normally `abstract` is used in documents typeset with the article document class.

```
\begin{abstract}
The abstract abstract.
\end{abstract}
```

> The abstract abstract.

2.11.5 Printing Verbatim

Text that is enclosed between \begin{verbatim} and \end{verbatim} will
be directly printed, as if typed on a typewriter, with all line breaks and
spaces, without any LATEX command being executed.

Within a paragraph, similar behavior can be accessed with

```
\verb+text+
```

The + is just an example of a delimiter character. Use any character except
letters, * or space. Many LATEX examples in this booklet are typeset with
this command.

```
The \verb|\ldots| command \ldots

\begin{verbatim}
10 PRINT "HELLO WORLD ";
20 GOTO 10
\end{verbatim}
```

```
The \ldots command ...


10 PRINT "HELLO WORLD ";
20 GOTO 10
```

```
\begin{verbatim*}
the starred version of
the         verbatim
environment emphasizes
the spaces   in the text
\end{verbatim*}
```

```
the␣starred␣version␣of
the␣␣␣␣␣␣verbatim
environment␣emphasizes
the␣spaces␣␣␣in␣the␣text
```

The \verb command can be used in a similar fashion with a star:

```
\verb*|like    this :-) |
```

```
like␣␣␣this␣:-)␣
```

The verbatim environment and the \verb command may not be used
within parameters of other commands.

2.11.6 Tabular

The tabular environment can be used to typeset beautiful tables with
optional horizontal and vertical lines. LATEX determines the width of the
columns automatically.

The *table spec* argument of the

```
\begin{tabular}[pos]{table spec}
```

command defines the format of the table. Use an `l` for a column of left-
aligned text, `r` for right-aligned text, and `c` for centred text; `p{width}`

for a column containing justified text with line breaks, and $\boxed{\texttt{|}}$ for a vertical line.

If the text in a column is too wide for the page, LaTeX won't automatically wrap it. Using $\boxed{\texttt{p\{width\}}}$ you can define a special type of column which will wrap-around the text as in a normal paragraph.

The *pos* argument specifies the vertical position of the table relative to the baseline of the surrounding text. Use one of the letters $\boxed{\texttt{t}}$, $\boxed{\texttt{b}}$ and $\boxed{\texttt{c}}$ to specify table alignment at the top, bottom or centre.

Within a `tabular` environment, `&` jumps to the next column, `\\` starts a new line and `\hline` inserts a horizontal line. Add partial lines by using `\cline{i-j}`, where *i* and *j* are the column numbers the line should extend over.

```
\begin{tabular}{|r|l|}
\hline
7C0 & hexadecimal \\
3700 & octal \\ \cline{2-2}
11111000000 & binary \\
\hline \hline
1984 & decimal \\
\hline
\end{tabular}
```

7C0	hexadecimal
3700	octal
11111000000	binary
1984	decimal

```
\begin{tabular}{|p{4.7cm}|}
\hline
Welcome to Boxy's paragraph.
We sincerely hope you'll
all enjoy the show.\\
\hline
\end{tabular}
```

Welcome to Boxy's paragraph. We sincerely hope you'll all enjoy the show.

The column separator can be specified with the $\boxed{\texttt{@\{...\}}}$ construct. This command kills the inter-column space and replaces it with whatever is between the curly braces. One common use for this command is explained below in the decimal alignment problem. Another possible application is to suppress leading space in a table with $\boxed{\texttt{@\{\}}}$.

```
\begin{tabular}{@{} l @{}}
\hline
no leading space\\
\hline
\end{tabular}
```

no leading space

```
\begin{tabular}{l}
\hline
leading space left and right\\
\hline
\end{tabular}
```

<u>leading space left and right</u>

Since there is no built-in way to align numeric columns to a decimal point,[24] we can "cheat" and do it by using two columns: a right-aligned integer and a left-aligned fraction. The @{.} command in the `\begin{tabular}` line replaces the normal inter-column spacing with just a ".", giving the appearance of a single, decimal-point-justified column. Don't forget to replace the decimal point in your numbers with a column separator (&)! A column label can be placed above our numeric "column" by using the `\multicolumn` command.

```
\begin{tabular}{c r @{.} l}
Pi expression          &
\multicolumn{2}{c}{Value} \\
\hline
$\pi$                  & 3&1416  \\
$\pi^{\pi}$            & 36&46   \\
$(\pi^{\pi})^{\pi}$ & 80662&7 \\
\end{tabular}
```

Pi expression	Value
π	3.1416
π^{π}	36.46
$(\pi^{\pi})^{\pi}$	80662.7

```
\begin{tabular}{|c|c|}
\hline
\multicolumn{2}{|c|}{Ene} \\
\hline
Mene & Muh! \\
\hline
\end{tabular}
```

Material typeset with the tabular environment always stays together on one page. If you want to typeset long tables, you might want to use the longtable environments.

Sometimes the default LaTeX tables do feel a bit cramped. So you may want to give them a bit more breathing space by setting a higher `\arraystretch` and `\tabcolsep` value.

---

[24]If the 'tools' bundle is installed on your system, have a look at the dcolumn package.

```
\begin{tabular}{|l|}
\hline
These lines\\\hline
are tight\\\hline
\end{tabular}

{\renewcommand{\arraystretch}{1.5}
\renewcommand{\tabcolsep}{0.2cm}
\begin{tabular}{|l|}
\hline
less cramped\\\hline
table layout\\\hline
\end{tabular}}
```

| These lines |
| are tight |

| less cramped |
| table layout |

If you just want to grow the height of a single row in your table add an invisible vertical bar[25]. Use a zero width \rule to implement this trick.

```
\begin{tabular}{|c|}
\hline
\rule{1pt}{4ex}Pitprop \ldots\\
\hline
\rule{0pt}{4ex}Strut\\
\hline
\end{tabular}
```

| Pitprop … |
| Strut |

The pt and ex in the example above are TEX units. Read more on units in table 6.5 on page 130.

A number of extra commands, enhancing the tabular environment are available in the booktabs package. It makes the creation of professional looking tables with proper spacing quite a bit simpler.

2.12   Floating Bodies

Today most publications contain a lot of figures and tables. These elements need special treatment, because they cannot be broken across pages. One method would be to start a new page every time a figure or a table is too large to fit on the present page. This approach would leave pages partially empty, which looks very bad.

The solution to this problem is to 'float' any figure or table that does not fit on the current page to a later page, while filling the current page with body text. LATEX offers two environments for floating bodies; one for tables and one for figures. To take full advantage of these two environments it is important to understand approximately how LATEX handles floats internally. Otherwise floats may become a major source of frustration, because LATEX never puts them where you want them to be.

---

[25]In professional typesetting, this is called a strut.

Let's first have a look at the commands LaTeX supplies for floats:

Any material enclosed in a `figure` or `table` environment will be treated as floating matter. Both float environments support an optional parameter

---

`\begin{figure}`[*placement specifier*] or `\begin{table}`[...]

---

called the *placement specifier*. This parameter is used to tell LaTeX about the locations to which the float is allowed to be moved. A *placement specifier* is constructed by building a string of *float-placing permissions*. See Table 2.9.

For example, a table could be started with the following line

`\begin{table}[!hbp]`

The placement specifier [`!hbp`] allows LaTeX to place the table right here (**h**) or at the bottom (**b**) of some page or on a special floats page (**p**), and all this even if it does not look that good (**!**). If no placement specifier is given, the standard classes assume [`tbp`].

LaTeX will place every float it encounters according to the placement specifier supplied by the author. If a float cannot be placed on the current page it is deferred either to the *figures* queue or the *tables* queue.[26] When a new page is started, LaTeX first checks if it is possible to fill a special 'float' page with floats from the queues. If this is not possible, the first float on each queue is treated as if it had just occurred in the text: LaTeX tries again to place it according to its respective placement specifiers (except 'h,' which is no longer possible). Any new floats occurring in the text get placed into the appropriate queues. LaTeX strictly maintains the original order of appearance for each type of float. That's why a figure that cannot be placed pushes all further figures to the end of the document. Therefore:

---

[26]These are FIFO—'first in first out'—queues!

Table 2.9: Float Placing Permissions.

Spec	Permission to place the float ...
h	*here* at the very place in the text where it occurred. This is useful mainly for small floats.
t	at the *top* of a page
b	at the *bottom* of a page
p	on a special *page* containing only floats.
!	without considering most of the internal parameters[a], which could otherwise stop this float from being placed.

---

[a]Such as the maximum number of floats allowed on one page.

If LaTeX is not placing the floats as you expected, it is often only one float jamming one of the two float queues.

While it is possible to give LaTeX single-location placement specifiers, this causes problems. If the float does not fit in the location specified it becomes stuck, blocking subsequent floats. In particular, you should never, ever use the [h] option—it is so bad that in more recent versions of LaTeX, it is automatically replaced by [ht].

Having explained the difficult bit, there are some more things to mention about the `table` and `figure` environments. Use the

```
\caption{caption text}
```

command to define a caption for the float. A running number and the string "Figure" or "Table" will be added by LaTeX.

The two commands

```
\listoffigures and \listoftables
```

operate analogously to the `\tableofcontents` command, printing a list of figures or tables, respectively. These lists will display the whole caption, so if you tend to use long captions you must have a shorter version of the caption for the lists. This is accomplished by entering the short version in brackets after the `\caption` command.

```
\caption[Short]{LLLLLLooooooonnnnnggggg}
```

Use `\label` and `\ref` to create a reference to a float within your text. Note that the `\label` command must come *after* the `\caption` command since you want it to reference the number of the caption.

The following example draws a square and inserts it into the document. You could use this if you wanted to reserve space for images you are going to paste into the finished document.

```
Figure~\ref{white} is an example of Pop-Art.
\begin{figure}[!hbtp]
\makebox[\textwidth]{\framebox[5cm]{\rule{0pt}{5cm}}}
\caption{Five by Five in Centimetres.\label{white}}
\end{figure}
```

In the example above, LaTeX will try *really hard* (!) to place the figure right *here* (h).[27] If this is not possible, it tries to place the figure at the *bottom* (b) of the page. Failing to place the figure on the current page, it determines

---

[27] assuming the figure queue is empty.

whether it is possible to create a float page containing this figure and maybe some tables from the tables queue. If there is not enough material for a special float page, LATEX starts a new page, and once more treats the figure as if it had just occurred in the text.

Under certain circumstances it might be necessary to use the

> `\clearpage` or even the `\cleardoublepage`

command. It orders LATEX to immediately place all floats remaining in the queues and then start a new page. `\cleardoublepage` even goes to a new right-hand page.

You will learn how to include POSTSCRIPT drawings in your LATEX 2$_\varepsilon$ documents later in this introduction.

2.13 Protecting Fragile Commands

Text given as arguments of commands like `\caption` or `\section` may show up more than once in the document (e.g. in the table of contents as well as in the body of the document). Some commands will break when used in the argument of `\section`-like commands. Compilation of your document will fail. These commands are called fragile commands—for example, `\footnote` or `\phantom`. These fragile commands need protection (don't we all?). Protect them by putting the `\protect` command in front of them. Now they will work properly even when used in moving arguments.

`\protect` only affects the next command, not even to its arguments. In most cases a superfluous `\protect` won't hurt.

```
\section{I am considerate
        \protect\footnote{and protect my footnotes}}
```

Chapter 3

Typesetting Mathematical Formulae

Now you are ready! In this chapter, we will attack the main strength of TeX: mathematical typesetting. But be warned, this chapter only scratches the surface. While the things explained here are sufficient for many people, don't despair if you can't find a solution to your mathematical typesetting needs here. It is highly likely that your problem is addressed in $\mathcal{AMS}$-LaTeX.

3.1 The $\mathcal{AMS}$-LaTeX bundle

If you want to typeset (advanced) mathematics, you should use $\mathcal{AMS}$-LaTeX. The $\mathcal{AMS}$-LaTeX bundle is a collection of packages and classes for mathematical typesetting. We will mostly deal with the amsmath package which is a part of the bundle. $\mathcal{AMS}$-LaTeX is produced by The *American Mathematical Society* and it is used extensively for mathematical typesetting. LaTeX itself does provide some basic features and environments for mathematics, but they are limited (or maybe it's the other way around: $\mathcal{AMS}$-LaTeX is *unlimited*!) and in some cases inconsistent.

$\mathcal{AMS}$-LaTeX is a part of the required distribution and is provided with all recent LaTeX distributions.[1] In this chapter, we assume amsmath is loaded in the preamble; \usepackage{amsmath}.

3.2 Single Equations

A mathematical formula can be typeset in-line within a paragraph (*text style*), or the paragraph can be broken and the formula typeset separately (*display style*). Mathematical equations *within* a paragraph are entered between \$ and \$:

---

[1] If yours is missing it, go to `CTAN://pkg/amslatex`.

```
Add $a$ squared and $b$ squared
to get $c$ squared. Or, using
a more mathematical approach:
$a^2 + b^2 = c^2$
```

Add a squared and b squared to get c squared. Or, using a more mathematical approach: $a^2 + b^2 = c^2$

```
\TeX{} is pronounced as
$\tau\epsilon\chi$\\[5pt]
100~m$^{3}$ of water\\[5pt]
This comes from my $\heartsuit$
```

TeX is pronounced as $\tau\epsilon\chi$

100 m^3 of water

This comes from my $\heartsuit$

If you want your larger equations to be set apart from the rest of the paragraph, it is preferable to *display* them rather than to break the paragraph apart. To do this, you enclose them between \begin{equation} and \end{equation}.[2] You can then \label an equation number and refer to it somewhere else in the text by using the \eqref command. If you want to name the equation something specific, you \tag it instead.

```
Add $a$ squared and $b$ squared
to get $c$ squared. Or, using
a more mathematical approach
 \begin{equation}
   a^2 + b^2 = c^2
 \end{equation}
Einstein says
 \begin{equation}
   E = mc^2 \label{clever}
 \end{equation}
He didn't say
 \begin{equation}
   1 + 1 = 3 \tag{dumb}
 \end{equation}
This is a reference to
\eqref{clever}.
```

Add a squared and b squared to get c squared. Or, using a more mathematical approach

$$a^2 + b^2 = c^2 \qquad (3.1)$$

Einstein says

$$E = mc^2 \qquad (3.2)$$

He didn't say

$$1 + 1 = 3 \qquad \text{(dumb)}$$

This is a reference to (3.2).

If you don't want LATEX to number the equations, use the starred version of `equation` using an asterisk, `equation*`, or even easier, enclose the equation in \[and \]:[3]

---

[2]This is an amsmath command. If you don't have access to the package for some obscure reason, you can use LATEX's own `displaymath` environment instead.

[3] This is again from amsmath. Standard LATEX's has only the `equation` environment without the star.

```
Add $a$ squared and $b$ squared
to get $c$ squared. Or, using
a more mathematical approach
 \begin{equation*}
   a^2 + b^2 = c^2
 \end{equation*}
or you can type less for the
same effect:
 \[ a^2 + b^2 = c^2 \]
```

Add a squared and b squared to get c squared. Or, using a more mathematical approach

$$a^2 + b^2 = c^2$$

or you can type less for the same effect:

$$a^2 + b^2 = c^2$$

While \[is short and sweet, it does not allow switching between numbered and not numbered style as easily as `equation` and `equation*`.

Note the difference in typesetting style between text style and display style equations:

```
This is text style:
$\lim_{n \to \infty}
 \sum_{k=1}^n \frac{1}{k^2}
 = \frac{\pi^2}{6}$.
And this is display style:
 \begin{equation}
   \lim_{n \to \infty}
   \sum_{k=1}^n \frac{1}{k^2}
   = \frac{\pi^2}{6}
 \end{equation}
```

This is text style: $\lim_{n \to \infty} \sum_{k=1}^n \frac{1}{k^2} = \frac{\pi^2}{6}$. And this is display style:

$$\lim_{n \to \infty} \sum_{k=1}^n \frac{1}{k^2} = \frac{\pi^2}{6} \tag{3.3}$$

In text style, enclose tall or deep math expressions or sub expressions in \smash. This makes LaTeX ignore the height of these expressions. This keeps the line spacing even.

```
A $d_{e_{e_p}}$ mathematical
expression  followed by a
$h^{i^{g^h}}$ expression. As
opposed to a smashed
\smash{$d_{e_{e_p}}$} expression
followed by a
\smash{$h^{i^{g^h}}$} expression.
```

A $d_{e_{e_p}}$ mathematical expression followed by a $h^{i^{g^h}}$ expression. As opposed to a smashed $d_{e_{e_p}}$ expression followed by a $h^{i^{g^h}}$ expression.

3.2.1   Math Mode

There are also differences between *math mode* and *text mode*. For example, in *math mode*:

1. Most spaces and line breaks do not have any significance, as all spaces are either derived logically from the mathematical expressions, or have to be specified with special commands such as \, , \quad or \qquad (we'll get back to that later, see section 3.7).

2. Empty lines are not allowed. Only one paragraph per formula.

3. Each letter is considered to be the name of a variable and will be typeset as such. If you want to typeset normal text within a formula (normal upright font and normal spacing) then you have to enter the text using the \text{...} command (see also section 3.8 on page 70).

```
$\forall x \in \mathbf{R}:
 \qquad x^{2} \geq 0$
```

$$\forall x \in \mathbf{R}: \qquad x^2 \geq 0$$

```
$x^{2} \geq 0\qquad
 \text{for all }x\in\mathbf{R}$
```

$$x^2 \geq 0 \qquad \text{for all } x \in \mathbf{R}$$

Mathematicians can be very fussy about which symbols are used: it would be conventional here to use the 'blackboard bold' font, which is obtained using \mathbb from the package amssymb.[4] The last example becomes

```
$x^{2} \geq 0\qquad
 \text{for all } x
 \in \mathbb{R}$
```

$$x^2 \geq 0 \qquad \text{for all } x \in \mathbb{R}$$

See Table 3.14 on page 79 and Table 6.4 on page 125 for more math fonts.

3.3 Building Blocks of a Mathematical Formula

In this section, we describe the most important commands used in mathematical typesetting. Most of the commands in this section will not require amsmath (if they do, it will be stated clearly), but load it anyway.

Lowercase Greek letters are entered as \alpha, \beta, \gamma, ..., uppercase letters are entered as \Gamma, \Delta, ...[5]

Take a look at Table 3.2 on page 75 for a list of Greek letters.

```
$\lambda,\xi,\pi,\theta,
 \mu,\Phi,\Omega,\Delta$
```

$$\lambda, \xi, \pi, \theta, \mu, \Phi, \Omega, \Delta$$

Exponents, Superscripts and Subscripts can be specified using the ^ and the _ characters. Most math mode commands act only on the next character, so if you want a command to affect several characters, you have to group them together using curly braces: {...}.

---

[4]amssymb is not a part of the $\mathcal{AMS}$-LaTeX bundle, but it is perhaps still a part of your LaTeX distribution. Check your distribution or go to CTAN:/fonts/amsfonts/latex/ to obtain it.

[5]There is no uppercase Alpha, Beta etc. defined in LaTeX 2_ε because it looks the same as a normal roman A, B...

Table 3.3 on page 76 lists a lot of binary relations like $\subseteq$ and $\perp$.

```
$p^3_{ij} \qquad
 m_\text{Knuth}\qquad
\sum_{k=1}^3 k \\[5pt]
 a^x+y \neq a^{x+y}\qquad
 e^{x^2} \neq {e^x}^2$
```

$$p_{ij}^3 \qquad m_{\text{Knuth}} \qquad \sum_{k=1}^3 k$$
$$a^x + y \neq a^{x+y} \qquad e^{x^2} \neq e^{x2}$$

The **square root** is entered as `\sqrt`; the nth root is generated with
`\sqrt[n]`. The size of the root sign is determined automatically by LaTeX.
If just the sign is needed, use `\surd`.

See various kinds of arrows like $\hookrightarrow$ and $\rightleftharpoons$ on Table 3.6 on page 77.

```
$\sqrt{x} \Leftrightarrow x^{1/2}
 \quad \sqrt[3]{2}
 \quad \sqrt{x^{2} + \sqrt{y}}
 \quad \surd[x^2 + y^2]$
```

$$\sqrt{x} \Leftrightarrow x^{1/2} \quad \sqrt[3]{2} \quad \sqrt{x^2 + \sqrt{y}} \quad \surd[x^2 + y^2]$$

While the **dot** sign to indicate the multiplication operation is normally
left out, it is sometimes written to help the eye in grouping a formula. Use
`\cdot` to typeset a single centered dot. `\cdots` is three centered **dots** while
`\ldots` sets the dots low (on the baseline). Besides that, there are `\vdots`
for vertical and `\ddots` for diagonal dots. There are more examples in
section 3.6.

```
$\Psi = v_1 \cdot v_2
 \cdot \ldots \qquad
 n! = 1 \cdot 2
 \cdots (n-1) \cdot n$
```

$$\Psi = v_1 \cdot v_2 \cdot \ldots \qquad n! = 1 \cdot 2 \cdots (n-1) \cdot n$$

The commands `\overline` and `\underline` create **horizontal lines**
directly over or under an expression:

```
$0.\overline{3} =
 \underline{\underline{1/3}}$
```

$$0.\overline{3} = \underline{\underline{1/3}}$$

The commands `\overbrace` and `\underbrace` create long **horizontal
braces** over or under an expression:

```
$\underbrace{\overbrace{a+b+c}^6
 \cdot \overbrace{d+e+f}^7}
 _\text{meaning of life} = 42$
```

$$\underbrace{\overbrace{a+b+c}^6 \cdot \overbrace{d+e+f}^7}_{\text{meaning of life}} = 42$$

To add mathematical accents such as **small arrows** or **tilde** signs to
variables, the commands given in Table 3.1 on page 75 might be useful. Wide

hats and tildes covering several characters are generated with \widetilde and \widehat. Notice the difference between \hat and \widehat and the placement of \bar for a variable with subscript. The apostrophe mark ' gives a prime:

```
$f(x) = x^2 \qquad f'(x)
= 2x \qquad f''(x) = 2\\[5pt]
\hat{XY} \quad \widehat{XY}
\quad \bar{x_0} \quad \bar{x}_0$
```

$$f(x) = x^2 \qquad f'(x) = 2x \qquad f''(x) = 2$$
$$\hat{XY} \quad \widehat{XY} \quad \bar{x_0} \quad \bar{x}_0$$

Vectors are often specified by adding small arrow symbols on the tops of variables. This is done with the \vec command. The two commands \overrightarrow and \overleftarrow are useful to denote the vector from A to B:

```
$\vec{a} \qquad
\vec{AB} \qquad
\overrightarrow{AB}$
```

$$\vec{a} \qquad \vec{AB} \qquad \overrightarrow{AB}$$

Names of functions are often typeset in an upright font, and not in italics as variables are, so LaTeX supplies the following commands to typeset the most common function names:

\arccos	\cos	\csc	\exp	\ker	\limsup
\arcsin	\cosh	\deg	\gcd	\lg	\ln
\arctan	\cot	\det	\hom	\lim	\log
\arg	\coth	\dim	\inf	\liminf	\max
\sinh	\sup	\tan	\tanh	\min	\Pr
\sec	\sin				

```
\begin{equation*}
  \lim_{x \rightarrow 0}
    \frac{\sin x}{x}=1
\end{equation*}
```

$$\lim_{x \to 0} \frac{\sin x}{x} = 1$$

For functions missing from the list, use the \DeclareMathOperator command. There is even a starred version for functions with limits. This command works only in the preamble so the commented lines in the example below must be put into the preamble.

```
%\DeclareMathOperator{\argh}{argh}
%\DeclareMathOperator*{\nut}{Nut}
\begin{equation*}
  3\argh = 2\nut_{x=1}
\end{equation*}
```

$$3\operatorname{argh} = 2\operatorname*{Nut}_{x=1}$$

For the modulo function, there are two commands: \bmod for the binary operator "$a \bmod b$" and \pmod for expressions such as "$x \equiv a \pmod{b}$:"

```
$a\bmod b \\
 x\equiv a \pmod{b}$
```

$a \bmod b$
$x \equiv a \pmod{b}$

A built-up **fraction** is typeset with the `\frac{...}{...}` command. In in-line equations, the fraction is shrunk to fit the line. This style is obtainable in display style with `\tfrac`. The reverse, i.e. display style fraction in text, is made with `\dfrac`. Often the slashed form $1/2$ is preferable, because it looks better for small amounts of 'fraction material:'

```
In display style:
\begin{equation*}
  3/8 \qquad \frac{3}{8}
  \qquad \tfrac{3}{8}
\end{equation*}
```

In display style:

$$3/8 \qquad \frac{3}{8} \qquad \tfrac{3}{8}$$

```
In text style:
$1\frac{1}{2}$~hours \qquad
$1\dfrac{1}{2}$~hours
```

In text style: $1\frac{1}{2}$ hours $\qquad 1\dfrac{1}{2}$ hours

Here the `\partial` command for partial derivatives is used:

```
\begin{equation*}
  \sqrt{\frac{x^2}{k+1}}\qquad
  x^\frac{2}{k+1}\qquad
  \frac{\partial^2f}
  {\partial x^2}
\end{equation*}
```

$$\sqrt{\frac{x^2}{k+1}} \qquad x^{\frac{2}{k+1}} \qquad \frac{\partial^2 f}{\partial x^2}$$

To typeset binomial coefficients or similar structures, use the command `\binom` from `amsmath`:

```
Pascal's rule is
\begin{equation*}
 \binom{n}{k} =\binom{n-1}{k}
 + \binom{n-1}{k-1}
\end{equation*}
```

Pascal's rule is

$$\binom{n}{k} = \binom{n-1}{k} + \binom{n-1}{k-1}$$

For binary relations it may be useful to stack symbols over each other. `\stackrel{#1}{#2}` puts the symbol given in #1 in superscript-like size over #2 which is set in its usual position.

```
\begin{equation*}
 f_n(x) \stackrel{*}{\approx} 1
\end{equation*}
```

$$f_n(x) \stackrel{*}{\approx} 1$$

The **integral operator** is generated with \int, the **sum operator** with \sum, and the **product operator** with \prod. The upper and lower limits are specified with ^ and _ like subscripts and superscripts:

```
\begin{equation*}
\sum_{i=1}^n \qquad
\int_0^{\frac{\pi}{2}} \qquad
\prod_\epsilon
\end{equation*}
```

$$\sum_{i=1}^n \qquad \int_0^{\frac{\pi}{2}} \qquad \prod_\epsilon$$

To get more control over the placement of indices in complex expressions, amsmath provides the \substack command:

```
\begin{equation*}
\sum^n_{\substack{0<i<n \\
        j\subseteq i}}
  P(i,j) = Q(i,j)
\end{equation*}
```

$$\sum_{\substack{0<i<n \\ j\subseteq i}}^n P(i,j) = Q(i,j)$$

LaTeX provides all sorts of symbols for **bracketing** and other **delimiters** (e.g. [⟨ ∥ ↕). Round and square brackets can be entered with the corresponding keys and curly braces with \{, but all other delimiters are generated with special commands (e.g. \updownarrow).

```
\begin{equation*}
{a,b,c} \neq \{a,b,c\}
\end{equation*}
```

$$a,b,c \neq \{a,b,c\}$$

If you put \left in front of an opening delimiter and \right in front of a closing delimiter, LaTeX will automatically determine the correct size of the delimiter. Note that you must close every \left with a corresponding \right. If you don't want anything on the right, use the invisible "\right.":

```
\begin{equation*}
1 + \left(\frac{1}{1-x^{2}}
    \right)^3 \qquad
\left. \ddagger \frac{~}{~}\right)
\end{equation*}
```

$$1 + \left(\frac{1}{1-x^2}\right)^3 \qquad \left. \ddagger \frac{~}{~}\right)$$

In some cases it is necessary to specify the correct size of a mathematical delimiter by hand, which can be done using the commands \big, \Big, \bigg and \Bigg as prefixes to most delimiter commands:

```
$\Big((x+1)(x-1)\Big)^{2}$\\
$\big( \Big( \bigg( \Bigg( \quad
\big\} \Big\} \bigg\} \Bigg\} \quad
\big\| \Big\| \bigg\| \Bigg\| \quad
\big\Downarrow \Big\Downarrow
\bigg\Downarrow \Bigg\Downarrow$
```

$$\Big((x+1)(x-1)\Big)^2$$
$$\big(\Big(\bigg(\Bigg(\quad \big\} \Big\} \bigg\} \Bigg\} \quad \big\| \Big\| \bigg\| \Bigg\| \quad \big\Downarrow \Big\Downarrow \bigg\Downarrow \Bigg\Downarrow$$

For a list of all delimiters available, see Table 3.8 on page 78.

3.4 Single Equations that are Too Long: multline

If an equation is too long, we have to wrap it somehow. Unfortunately, wrapped equations are usually less easy to read than not wrapped ones. To improve the readability, there are certain rules on how to do the wrapping:

1. In general one should always wrap an equation **before** an equality sign or an operator.

2. A wrap before an equality sign is preferable to a wrap before any operator.

3. A wrap before a plus- or minus-operator is preferable to a wrap before a multiplication-operator.

4. Any other type of wrap should be avoided if at all possible.

The easiest way to achieve such a wrapping is the use of the `multline` environment:[6]

```
\begin{multline}
  a + b + c + d + e + f
  + g + h + i
  \\
  = j + k + l + m + n
\end{multline}
```

$$a + b + c + d + e + f + g + h + i$$
$$= j + k + l + m + n \quad (3.4)$$

The difference from the `equation` environment is that an arbitrary line-break (or also multiple line-breaks) can be introduced. This is done by putting a `\\` on those places where the equation needs to be wrapped. Similarly to `equation*` there also exists a `multline*` version for preventing an equation number.

Often the `IEEEeqnarray` environment (see section 3.5) will yield better results. Consider the following situation:

```
\begin{equation}
  a = b + c + d + e + f
  + g + h + i + j
  + k + l + m + n + o + p
  \label{eq:equation_too_long}
\end{equation}
```

$$a = b+c+d+e+f+g+h+i+j+k+l+m+n+o+p$$
$$(3.5)$$

Here it is actually the RHS that is too long to fit on one line. The `multline` environment creates the following output:

---

[6]The `multline`-environment is from `amsmath`.

```
\begin{multline}
  a = b + c + d + e + f
  + g + h + i + j \\
  + k + l + m + n + o + p
\end{multline}
```

$$a = b + c + d + e + f + g + h + i + j$$
$$+ k + l + m + n + o + p \quad (3.6)$$

This is better than (3.5), but it has the disadvantage that the equality sign loses its natural greater importance with respect to the plus operator in front of k. The better solution is provided by the IEEEeqnarray environment that will be discussed in detail in Section 3.5.

3.5   Multiple Equations

In the most general situation we have a sequence of several equalities that do not fit onto one line. Here we need to work with vertical alignment in order to keep the array of equations in a nice and readable structure.

Before we offer our suggestions on how to do this, we start with a few bad examples that show the biggest drawbacks of some common solutions.

3.5.1   Problems with Traditional Commands

To group multiple equations the align environment[7] could be used:

```
\begin{align}
  a & = b + c \\
  & = d + e
\end{align}
```

$$a = b + c \qquad\qquad (3.7)$$
$$= d + e \qquad\qquad (3.8)$$

this approach fails once a single line is too long:

```
\begin{align}
  a & = b + c \\
  & = d + e + f + g + h + i
  + j + k + l \nonumber \\
  & + m + n + o \\
  & = p + q + r + s
\end{align}
```

$$a = b + c \qquad\qquad\qquad (3.9)$$
$$= d + e + f + g + h + i + j + k + l$$
$$+ m + n + o \qquad\qquad (3.10)$$
$$= p + q + r + s \qquad\qquad (3.11)$$

Here $+ m$ should be below d and not below the equality sign. Of course, one could add some space (\hspace{...}), but this will never yield a precise arrangement (and is bad style...).

A better solution is offered by the eqnarray environment:

---

[7]The align-environment can also be used to group several blocks of equations beside each other. Another excellent use case for the IEEEeqnarray environment. Try an argument like {rCl+rCl}.

```
\begin{eqnarray}
  a & = & b + c \\
  & = & d + e + f + g + h + i
  + j + k + l \nonumber \\
  && +\: m + n + o \\
  & = & p + q + r + s
\end{eqnarray}
```

$$
\begin{array}{rcl}
a & = & b+c \hspace{2em} (3.12) \\
  & = & d+e+f+g+h+i+j+k+l \\
  &   & +\,m+n+o \hspace{1em} (3.13) \\
  & = & p+q+r+s \hspace{1em} (3.14)
\end{array}
$$

This is still not optimal. The spaces around the equality signs are too big. Particularly, they are **not** the same as in the `multline` and `equation` environments:

```
\begin{eqnarray}
  a & = & a = a
\end{eqnarray}
```

$$
a \quad = \quad a = a \hspace{2em} (3.15)
$$

...and the expression sometimes overlaps with the equation number even though there would be enough room on the left:

```
\begin{eqnarray}
  a & = & b + c
  \\
  & = & d + e + f + g + h^2
  + i^2 + j
  \label{eq:faultyeqnarray}
\end{eqnarray}
```

$$
\begin{array}{rcl}
a & = & b+c \hspace{3em} (3.16) \\
  & = & d+e+f+g+h^2+i^2+j \hspace{-0.5em}(3.17)
\end{array}
$$

While the environment offers a command `\lefteqn` that can be used when the LHS is too long:

```
\begin{eqnarray}
  \lefteqn{a + b + c + d
  + e + f + g + h}\nonumber\\
  & = & i + j + k + l + m
  \\
  & = & n + o + p + q + r + s
\end{eqnarray}
```

$$
\begin{array}{rcl}
\multicolumn{3}{l}{a+b+c+d+e+f+g+h} \\
  & = & i+j+k+l+m \hspace{1em} (3.18) \\
  & = & n+o+p+q+r+s \hspace{0.5em} (3.19)
\end{array}
$$

This is not optimal either as the RHS is too short and the array is not properly centered:

```
\begin{eqnarray}
  \lefteqn{a + b + c + d
  + e + f + g + h}
  \nonumber \\
  & = & i + j
\end{eqnarray}
```

$$
\begin{array}{rcl}
\multicolumn{3}{l}{a+b+c+d+e+f+g+h} \\
  & = & i+j \hspace{2em} (3.20)
\end{array}
$$

Having badmouthed the competition sufficiently, I can now steer you gently towards the glorious ...

3.5.2   IEEEeqnarray Environment

The IEEEeqnarray environment is a very powerful command with many options. Here, we will only introduce its basic functionalities. For more information please refer to the manual.[8]

First of all, in order to be able to use the IEEEeqnarray environment one needs to load the package[9] IEEEtrantools. Include the following line in the header of your document:

```
\usepackage[retainorgcmds]{IEEEtrantools}
```

The strength of IEEEeqnarray is the ability to specify the number of *columns* in the equation array. Usually, this specification will be {rCl}, *i.e.*, three columns, the first column right-justified, the middle one centered with a little more space around it (therefore we specify capital C instead of lower-case c) and the third column left-justified:

```
\begin{IEEEeqnarray}{rCl}
  a & = & b + c
  \\
  & = & d + e + f + g + h
  + i + j + k \nonumber\\
  && \negmedspace {} + l + m + n + o
  \\
  & = & p + q + r + s
\end{IEEEeqnarray}
```

$$a = b + c \qquad\qquad (3.21)$$
$$= d + e + f + g + h + i + j + k$$
$$+ l + m + n + o \qquad (3.22)$$
$$= p + q + r + s \qquad\qquad (3.23)$$

Any number of columns can be specified: {c} will give only one column with all entries centered, or {rCll} would add a fourth, left-justified column to use for comments. Moreover, beside l, c, r, L, C, R for math mode entries there are also s, t, u for left, centered, and right text mode entries. Additional space can be added with . and / and ? in increasing order.[10] Note the spaces around the equality signs in contrast to the space produced by the eqnarray environment.

3.5.3   Common Usage

In the following we will describe how we use IEEEeqnarray to solve the most common problems.

If a line overlaps with the equation number as in (3.17), the command

---

[8]The official manual is called CTAN://macros/latex/contrib/IEEEtran/IEEEtran_ HOWTO.pdf. The part about **IEEEeqnarray** can be found in Appendix F.

[9]The **IEEEtrantools** package may not be included in your setup, it can be found on CTAN.

[10]For more spacing types refer to Section 3.9.1.

```
\IEEEeqnarraynumspace
```

can be used: it has to be added in the corresponding line and makes sure that the whole equation array is shifted by the size of the equation numbers (the shift depends on the size of the number!): instead of

```
\begin{IEEEeqnarray}{rCl}
   a & = & b + c
   \\
   & = & d + e + f + g + h
   + i + j + k
   \\
   & = & l + m + n
\end{IEEEeqnarray}
```

$$a = b + c \qquad\qquad (3.24)$$
$$= d + e + f + g + h + i + j + (3.25)$$
$$= l + m + n \qquad\qquad (3.26)$$

we get

```
\begin{IEEEeqnarray}{rCl}
   a & = & b + c
   \\
   & = & d + e + f + g + h
   + i + j + k
   \IEEEeqnarraynumspace\\
   & = & l + m + n.
\end{IEEEeqnarray}
```

$$a = b + c \qquad\qquad (3.27)$$
$$= d + e + f + g + h + i + j + k \quad (3.28)$$
$$= l + m + n. \qquad\qquad (3.29)$$

If the LHS is too long, as a replacement for the faulty \lefteqn command, IEEEeqnarray offers the \IEEEeqnarraymulticol command which works in all situations:

```
\begin{IEEEeqnarray}{rCl}
   \IEEEeqnarraymulticol{3}{l}{
     a + b + c + d + e + f
     + g + h
   }\nonumber\\ \quad
   & = & i + j
   \\
   & = & k + l + m
\end{IEEEeqnarray}
```

$$a + b + c + d + e + f + g + h$$
$$= i + j \qquad\qquad (3.30)$$
$$= k + l + m \qquad\qquad (3.31)$$

The usage is identical to the \multicolumns command in the tabular-environment. The first argument {3} specifies that three columns shall be combined into one which will be left-justified {l}.

Note that by inserting \quad commands one can easily adapt the depth of the equation signs,[11] *e.g.*,

---

[11] I think that one quad is the distance that looks good for most cases.

```
\begin{IEEEeqnarray}{rCl}
  \IEEEeqnarraymulticol{3}{l}{
    a + b + c + d + e + f
    + g + h
  }\nonumber\\ \qquad\qquad
  & = & i + j
  \\
  & = & k + l + m
\end{IEEEeqnarray}
```

$$a + b + c + d + e + f + g + h$$
$$= i + j \qquad (3.32)$$
$$= k + l + m \qquad (3.33)$$

If an equation is split into two or more lines, LaTeX interprets the first $+$ or $-$ as a sign instead of operator. Therefore, it is necessary to add an additional space \: between the operator and the term: instead of

```
\begin{IEEEeqnarray}{rCl}
  a & = & b + c
  \\
  & = & d + e + f + g + h
  + i + j + k \nonumber\\
  && + l + m + n + o
  \\
  & = & p + q + r + s
\end{IEEEeqnarray}
```

$$a = b + c \qquad (3.34)$$
$$= d + e + f + g + h + i + j + k$$
$$+ l + m + n + o \qquad (3.35)$$
$$= p + q + r + s \qquad (3.36)$$

we should write

```
\begin{IEEEeqnarray}{rCl}
  a & = & b + c
  \\
  & = & d + e + f + g + h
  + i + j + k \nonumber\\
  && \negmedspace {} + l + m + n + o
  \\
  & = & p + q + r + s
\end{IEEEeqnarray}
```

$$a = b + c \qquad (3.37)$$
$$= d + e + f + g + h + i + j + k$$
$$+ l + m + n + o \qquad (3.38)$$
$$= p + q + r + s \qquad (3.39)$$

Note the space difference between $+$ and l! The construction {} + l forces the +-sign to be a binary operator rather than just a sign, and the unwanted ensuing space between {} and + is compensated by a negative medium space \negmedspace.

If a particular line should not have an equation number, the number can be suppressed using \nonumber (or \IEEEnonumber). If on such a line a label \label{eq:...} is defined, then this label is passed on to the next equation number that is not suppressed. Place the labels right before the line-break \\ or the next to the equation it belongs to. Apart from improving the readability of the source code this prevents a compilation error when a \IEEEmulticol command follows the label-definition.

There also exists a *-version where all equation numbers are suppressed. In this case an equation number can be made to appear using the command `\IEEEyesnumber`:

```
\begin{IEEEeqnarray*}{rCl}
  a & = & b + c \\
    & = & d + e \IEEEyesnumber\\
    & = & f + g
\end{IEEEeqnarray*}
```

$$
\begin{aligned}
a &= b + c \\
  &= d + e \\
  &= f + g
\end{aligned}
\qquad (3.40)
$$

Sub-numbers are also easily possible using `\IEEEyessubnumber`:

```
\begin{IEEEeqnarray}{rCl}
  a & = & b + c
  \IEEEyessubnumber\\
    & = & d + e
  \nonumber\\
    & = & f + g
  \IEEEyessubnumber
\end{IEEEeqnarray}
```

$$
\begin{aligned}
a &= b + c &\qquad (3.40a) \\
  &= d + e \\
  &= f + g &\qquad (3.40b)
\end{aligned}
$$

3.6   Arrays and Matrices

To typeset **arrays**, use the `array` environment. It works in a similar way to the `tabular` environment. The `\\` command is used to break the lines:

```
\begin{equation*}
  \mathbf{X} = \left(
    \begin{array}{ccc}
      x_1 & x_2 & \ldots \\
      x_3 & x_4 & \ldots \\
      \vdots & \vdots & \ddots
    \end{array} \right)
\end{equation*}
```

$$
\mathbf{X} = \left(
\begin{array}{ccc}
x_1 & x_2 & \ldots \\
x_3 & x_4 & \ldots \\
\vdots & \vdots & \ddots
\end{array} \right)
$$

The `array` environment can also be used to typeset piecewise functions by using a ". " as an invisible `\right` delimiter:

```
\begin{equation*}
  |x| = \left\{
    \begin{array}{rl}
      -x & \text{if } x < 0,\\
      0 & \text{if } x = 0,\\
      x & \text{if } x > 0.
    \end{array} \right.
\end{equation*}
```

$$
|x| = \left\{
\begin{array}{rl}
-x & \text{if } x < 0, \\
0 & \text{if } x = 0, \\
x & \text{if } x > 0.
\end{array} \right.
$$

The `cases` environment from `amsmath` simplifies the syntax, so it is worth a look:

```
\begin{equation*}
  |x| =
  \begin{cases}
    -x & \text{if } x < 0,\\
    0 & \text{if } x = 0,\\
    x & \text{if } x > 0.
  \end{cases}
\end{equation*}
```

$$|x| = \begin{cases} -x & \text{if } x < 0, \\ 0 & \text{if } x = 0, \\ x & \text{if } x > 0. \end{cases}$$

Matrices can be typeset by `array`, but `amsmath` provides a better solution using the different `matrix` environments. There are six versions with different delimiters: `matrix` (none), `pmatrix` (, `bmatrix` [, `Bmatrix` {, `vmatrix` | and `Vmatrix` ‖. You don't have to specify the number of columns as with `array`. The maximum number is 10, but it is customisable (though it is not very often you need 10 columns!):

```
\begin{equation*}
  \begin{matrix}
    1 & 2 \\
    3 & 4
  \end{matrix} \qquad
  \begin{bmatrix}
    p_{11} & p_{12} & \ldots
    & p_{1n} \\
    p_{21} & p_{22} & \ldots
    & p_{2n} \\
    \vdots & \vdots & \ddots
    & \vdots \\
    p_{m1} & p_{m2} & \ldots
    & p_{mn}
  \end{bmatrix}
\end{equation*}
```

$$\begin{matrix} 1 & 2 \\ 3 & 4 \end{matrix} \qquad \begin{bmatrix} p_{11} & p_{12} & \ldots & p_{1n} \\ p_{21} & p_{22} & \ldots & p_{2n} \\ \vdots & \vdots & \ddots & \vdots \\ p_{m1} & p_{m2} & \ldots & p_{mn} \end{bmatrix}$$

3.7 Spacing in Math Mode

If the spacing within formulae chosen by LaTeX is not satisfactory, it can be adjusted by inserting special spacing commands: `\,` for $\frac{3}{18}$ quad (⎵), `\:` for $\frac{4}{18}$ quad (⎵) and `\;` for $\frac{5}{18}$ quad (⎵). The escaped space character `\␣` generates a medium sized space comparable to the interword spacing and `\quad` (⎵) and `\qquad` (⎵) produce large spaces. The size of a `\quad` corresponds to the width of the character 'M' of the current font. `\!` produces a negative space of $-\frac{3}{18}$ quad (−⎵).

```
\begin{equation*}
  \int_1^2 \ln x \mathrm{d}x
  \qquad
  \int_1^2 \ln x \,\mathrm{d}x
\end{equation*}
```

$$\int_1^2 \ln x \mathrm{d}x \qquad \int_1^2 \ln x \, \mathrm{d}x$$

Note that 'd' in the differential is conventionally set in roman. In the next example, we define a new command \ud (upright d) which produces " d" (notice the spacing ⫿ before the d), so we don't have to write it every time. The \newcommand is placed in the preamble.

```
\newcommand{\ud}{\,\mathrm{d}}

\begin{equation*}
 \int_a^b f(x)\ud x
\end{equation*}
```

$$\int_a^b f(x) \, \mathrm{d}x$$

If you want to typeset multiple integrals, you'll discover that the spacing between the integrals is too wide. You can correct it using \!, but amsmath provides an easier way for fine-tuning the spacing, namely the \iint, \iiint, \iiiint, and \idotsint commands.

```
\newcommand{\ud}{\,\mathrm{d}}

\begin{IEEEeqnarray*}{c}
  \int\int f(x)g(y)
                   \ud x \ud y \\
  \int\!\!\!\int
        f(x)g(y) \ud x \ud y \\
  \iint f(x)g(y)  \ud x \ud y
\end{IEEEeqnarray*}
```

$$\int \int f(x)g(y) \, \mathrm{d}x \, \mathrm{d}y$$
$$\iint f(x)g(y) \, \mathrm{d}x \, \mathrm{d}y$$
$$\iint f(x)g(y) \, \mathrm{d}x \, \mathrm{d}y$$

See the electronic document testmath.tex (distributed with $\mathcal{AMS}$-LaTeX) or Chapter 8 of *The LaTeX Companion* [3] for further details.

3.7.1   Phantoms

When vertically aligning text using ^ and _ LaTeX is sometimes just a little too helpful. Using the \phantom command you can reserve space for characters that do not show up in the final output. The easiest way to understand this is to look at an example:

```
\begin{equation*}
{}^{14}_{6}\text{C}
\qquad \text{versus} \qquad
{}^{14}_{\phantom{1}6}\text{C}
\end{equation*}
```

$$^{14}_{6}\text{C} \qquad \text{versus} \qquad ^{14}_{6}\text{C}$$

If you want to typeset a lot of isotopes as in the example, the mhchem package is very useful for typesetting isotopes and chemical formulae too.

3.8   Fiddling with the Math Fonts

Different math fonts are listed on Table 3.14 on page 79.

```
$\Re \qquad
 \mathcal{R} \qquad
 \mathfrak{R} \qquad
 \mathbb{R} \qquad $
```

$$\Re \qquad \mathcal{R} \qquad \mathfrak{R} \qquad \mathbb{R}$$

The last two require **amssymb** or **amsfonts**.

Sometimes you need to tell LaTeX the correct font size. In math mode, this is set with the following four commands:

`\displaystyle` (123), `\textstyle` (123), `\scriptstyle` (123) and `\scriptscriptstyle` (123).

If $\sum$ is placed in a fraction, it'll be typeset in text style unless you tell LaTeX otherwise:

```
\begin{equation*}
 P = \frac{\displaystyle{
  \sum_{i=1}^n (x_i- x)
  (y_i- y)}}
  {\displaystyle{\left[
  \sum_{i=1}^n(x_i-x)^2
  \sum_{i=1}^n(y_i- y)^2
  \right]^{1/2}}}
\end{equation*}
```

$$P = \frac{\displaystyle\sum_{i=1}^n (x_i - x)(y_i - y)}{\displaystyle\left[\sum_{i=1}^n (x_i - x)^2 \sum_{i=1}^n (y_i - y)^2\right]^{1/2}}$$

Changing styles generally affects the way big operators and limits are displayed.

3.8.1   Bold Symbols

It is quite difficult to get bold symbols in LaTeX; this is probably intentional as amateur typesetters tend to overuse them. The font change command `\mathbf` gives bold letters, but these are roman (upright) whereas mathematical symbols are normally italic, and furthermore it doesn't work on lower case Greek letters. There is a `\boldmath` command, but *this can only be used outside math mode*. It works for symbols too, though:

```
$\mu, M \qquad
\mathbf{\mu}, \mathbf{M}$
\qquad \boldmath$\mu, M$}
```

$$\mu, M \qquad \mu, \mathbf{M} \qquad \boldsymbol{\mu, M}$$

The package amsbsy (included by amsmath) as well as the package bm from the tools bundle make this much easier as they include a \boldsymbol command:

```
$\mu, M \qquad
\boldsymbol{\mu}, \boldsymbol{M}$
```

$\mu, M \qquad \boldsymbol{\mu}, \boldsymbol{M}$

3.9 Theorems, Lemmas, ...

When writing mathematical documents, you probably need a way to typeset "Lemmas", "Definitions", "Axioms" and similar structures.

```
\newtheorem{name}[counter]{text}[section]
```

The *name* argument is a short keyword used to identify the "theorem". With the *text* argument you define the actual name of the "theorem", which will be printed in the final document.

The arguments in square brackets are optional. They are both used to specify the numbering used on the "theorem". Use the *counter* argument to specify the *name* of a previously declared "theorem". The new "theorem" will then be numbered in the same sequence. The *section* argument allows you to specify the sectional unit within which the "theorem" should get its numbers.

After executing the \newtheorem command in the preamble of your document, you can use the following command within the document.

```
\begin{name}[text]
This is my interesting theorem
\end{name}
```

The amsthm package (part of $\mathcal{A}\mathcal{M}\mathcal{S}$-LaTeX) provides the \theoremstyle{style} command which lets you define what the theorem is all about by picking from three predefined styles: definition (fat title, roman body), plain (fat title, italic body) or remark (italic title, roman body).

This should be enough theory. The following examples should remove any remaining doubt, and make it clear that the \newtheorem environment is way too complex to understand.

First define the theorems:

```
\theoremstyle{definition}  \newtheorem{law}{Law}
\theoremstyle{plain}       \newtheorem{jury}[law]{Jury}
\theoremstyle{remark}      \newtheorem*{marg}{Margaret}
```

```
\begin{law} \label{law:box}
Don't hide in the witness box
\end{law}
\begin{jury}[The Twelve]
It could be you! So beware and
see law~\ref{law:box}.\end{jury}
\begin{jury}
You will disregard the last
statement.\end{jury}
\begin{marg}No, No, No\end{marg}
\begin{marg}Denis!\end{marg}
```

> **Law 1.** Don't hide in the witness box
>
> **Jury 2** (The Twelve). *It could be you! So beware and see law 1.*
>
> **Jury 3.** *You will disregard the last statement.*
>
> *Margaret.* No, No, No
>
> *Margaret.* Denis!

The "Jury" theorem uses the same counter as the "Law" theorem, so it gets a number that is in sequence with the other "Laws". The argument in square brackets is used to specify a title or something similar for the theorem.

```
\newtheorem{mur}{Murphy}[section]

\begin{mur} If there are two or
more ways to do something, and
one of those ways can result in
a catastrophe, then someone
will do it.\end{mur}
```

> *Murphy* 3.9.1. If there are two or more ways to do something, and one of those ways can result in a catastrophe, then someone will do it.

The "Murphy" theorem gets a number that is linked to the number of the current section. You could also use another unit, for example chapter or subsection.

If you want to customize your theorems down to the last dot, the ntheorem package offers a plethora of options.

3.9.1 Proofs and End-of-Proof Symbol

The amsthm package also provides the proof environment.

```
\begin{proof}
 Trivial, use
 \begin{equation*}
   E=mc^2.
 \end{equation*}
\end{proof}
```

> *Proof.* Trivial, use
> $$E = mc^2.$$
> □

With the command \qedhere you can move the 'end of proof' symbol around for situations where it would end up alone on a line.

```
\begin{proof}
 Trivial, use
 \begin{equation*}
   E=mc^2. \qedhere
 \end{equation*}
\end{proof}
```

> *Proof.* Trivial, use
> $$E = mc^2.$$ □

Unfortunately, this correction does not work for IEEEeqnarray:

```
\begin{proof}
  This is a proof that ends
  with an equation array:
  \begin{IEEEeqnarray*}{rCl}
    a & = & b + c \\
    & = & d + e. \qedhere
  \end{IEEEeqnarray*}
\end{proof}
```

> *Proof.* This is a proof that ends with an equation array:
> $$a = b + c$$
> $$= d + e. □$$

The reason for this is the internal structure of IEEEeqnarray: it always puts two invisible columns at both sides of the array that only contain a stretchable space. By this IEEEeqnarray ensures that the equation array is horizontally centered. The \qedhere command should actually be put *outside* this stretchable space, but this does not happen as these columns are invisible to the user.

There is a very simple remedy. Define the stretching explicitly!

```
\begin{proof}
  This is a proof that ends
  with an equation array:
  \begin{IEEEeqnarray*}{+rCl+x*}
    a & = & b + c \\
    & = & d + e. & \qedhere
  \end{IEEEeqnarray*}
\end{proof}
```

> *Proof.* This is a proof that ends with an equation array:
> $$a = b + c$$
> $$= d + e.$$ □

Note that the + in {+rCl+x*} denotes stretchable spaces, one on the left of the equations (which, if not specified, will be done automatically by IEEEeqnarray!) and one on the right of the equations. But now on the right, *after* the stretching column, we add an empty column x. This column will only be needed on the last line if the \qedhere command is put there. Finally, we specify a *. This is a null-space that prevents IEEEeqnarray from adding another unwanted +-space!

In the case of equation numbering, there is a similar problem. Comparing

```
\begin{proof}
  This is a proof that ends
  with a numbered equation:
  \begin{equation}
    a = b + c.
  \end{equation}
\end{proof}
```

> *Proof.* This is a proof that ends with a numbered equation:
>
> $$a = b + c. \qquad\qquad (3.41)$$
>
> $\square$

with

```
\begin{proof}
  This is a proof that ends
  with a numbered equation:
  \begin{equation}
    a = b + c. \qedhere
  \end{equation}
\end{proof}
```

> *Proof.* This is a proof that ends with a numbered equation:
>
> $$a = b + c. \qquad\qquad (3.42)$$
> $\square$

you notice that in the (correct) second version the $\square$ is much closer to the equation than in the first version.

Similarly, the correct way of putting the QED-symbol at the end of an equation array is as follows:

```
\begin{proof}
  This is a proof that ends
  with an equation array:
  \begin{IEEEeqnarray}{+rCl+x*}
    a & = & b + c \\
      & = & d + e. \\
    &&& \qedhere\nonumber
  \end{IEEEeqnarray}
\end{proof}
```

> *Proof.* This is a proof that ends with an equation array:
>
> $$a = b + c \qquad\qquad (3.43)$$
> $$= d + e. \qquad\qquad (3.44)$$
> $\square$

which contrasts with

```
\begin{proof}
  This is a proof that ends
  with an equation array:
  \begin{IEEEeqnarray}{rCl}
    a & = & b + c \\
      & = & d + e.
  \end{IEEEeqnarray}
\end{proof}
```

> *Proof.* This is a proof that ends with an equation array:
>
> $$a = b + c \qquad\qquad (3.45)$$
> $$= d + e. \qquad\qquad (3.46)$$
>
> $\square$

3.10 List of Mathematical Symbols

The following tables demonstrate all the symbols normally accessible from *math mode*.

Note that some tables show symbols only accessible after loading the amssymb package in the preamble of your document[12]. If the $\mathcal{AMS}$ package and fonts are not installed on your system, have a look at `CTAN: pkg/amslatex`. An even more comprehensive list of symbols can be found at `CTAN:info/symbols/comprehensive`.

Table 3.1: Math Mode Accents.

$\hat{a}$	`\hat{a}`	$\check{a}$	`\check{a}`	$\tilde{a}$	`\tilde{a}`
$\grave{a}$	`\grave{a}`	$\dot{a}$	`\dot{a}`	$\ddot{a}$	`\ddot{a}`
$\bar{a}$	`\bar{a}`	$\vec{a}$	`\vec{a}`	$\widehat{AAA}$	`\widehat{AAA}`
$\acute{a}$	`\acute{a}`	$\breve{a}$	`\breve{a}`	$\widetilde{AAA}$	`\widetilde{AAA}`
$\mathring{a}$	`\mathring{a}`				

Table 3.2: Greek Letters.

There is no uppercase of some of the letters like `\Alpha`, `\Beta` and so on, because they look the same as normal roman letters: A, B. . .

α	`\alpha`	θ	`\theta`	o	`o`	υ	`\upsilon`
β	`\beta`	ϑ	`\vartheta`	π	`\pi`	ϕ	`\phi`
γ	`\gamma`	ι	`\iota`	ϖ	`\varpi`	φ	`\varphi`
δ	`\delta`	κ	`\kappa`	ρ	`\rho`	χ	`\chi`
ϵ	`\epsilon`	λ	`\lambda`	ϱ	`\varrho`	ψ	`\psi`
ε	`\varepsilon`	μ	`\mu`	σ	`\sigma`	ω	`\omega`
ζ	`\zeta`	ν	`\nu`	ς	`\varsigma`		
η	`\eta`	ξ	`\xi`	τ	`\tau`		
Γ	`\Gamma`	Λ	`\Lambda`	Σ	`\Sigma`	Ψ	`\Psi`
Δ	`\Delta`	Ξ	`\Xi`	Υ	`\Upsilon`	Ω	`\Omega`
Θ	`\Theta`	Π	`\Pi`	Φ	`\Phi`		

---

[12]The tables were derived from `symbols.tex` by David Carlisle and subsequently changed extensively as suggested by Josef Tkadlec.

Table 3.3: Binary Relations.

You can negate the following symbols by prefixing them with a \not command.

$<$	\<	$>$	\>	$=$	=
$\leq$	\leq or \le	$\geq$	\geq or \ge	$\equiv$	\equiv
$\ll$	\ll	$\gg$	\gg	$\doteq$	\doteq
$\prec$	\prec	$\succ$	\succ	$\sim$	\sim
$\preceq$	\preceq	$\succeq$	\succeq	$\simeq$	\simeq
$\subset$	\subset	$\supset$	\supset	$\approx$	\approx
$\subseteq$	\subseteq	$\supseteq$	\supseteq	$\cong$	\cong
$\sqsubset$	\sqsubset ^{a}	$\sqsupset$	\sqsupset ^{a}	$\Join$	\Join ^{a}
$\sqsubseteq$	\sqsubseteq	$\sqsupseteq$	\sqsupseteq	$\bowtie$	\bowtie
$\in$	\in	$\ni$	\ni , \owns	$\propto$	\propto
$\vdash$	\vdash	$\dashv$	\dashv	$\models$	\models
$\mid$	\mid	$\parallel$	\parallel	$\perp$	\perp
$\smile$	\smile	$\frown$	\frown	$\asymp$	\asymp
$:$	:	$\notin$	\notin	$\neq$	\neq or \ne

^{a}Use the latexsym package to access this symbol

Table 3.4: Binary Operators.

$+$	+	$-$	-		
$\pm$	\pm	$\mp$	\mp	$\triangleleft$	\triangleleft
$\cdot$	\cdot	$\div$	\div	$\triangleright$	\triangleright
$\times$	\times	$\setminus$	\setminus	$\star$	\star
$\cup$	\cup	$\cap$	\cap	$\ast$	\ast
$\sqcup$	\sqcup	$\sqcap$	\sqcap	$\circ$	\circ
$\vee$	\vee , \lor	$\wedge$	\wedge , \land	$\bullet$	\bullet
$\oplus$	\oplus	$\ominus$	\ominus	$\diamond$	\diamond
$\odot$	\odot	$\oslash$	\oslash	$\uplus$	\uplus
$\otimes$	\otimes	$\bigcirc$	\bigcirc	$\amalg$	\amalg
$\bigtriangleup$	\bigtriangleup	$\bigtriangledown$	\bigtriangledown	$\dagger$	\dagger
$\lhd$	\lhd ^{a}	$\rhd$	\rhd ^{a}	$\ddagger$	\ddagger
$\unlhd$	\unlhd ^{a}	$\unrhd$	\unrhd ^{a}	$\wr$	\wr

Table 3.5: BIG Operators.

$\sum$	\sum	$\bigcup$	\bigcup	$\bigvee$	\bigvee
$\prod$	\prod	$\bigcap$	\bigcap	$\bigwedge$	\bigwedge
$\coprod$	\coprod	$\bigsqcup$	\bigsqcup	$\biguplus$	\biguplus
$\int$	\int	$\oint$	\oint	$\bigodot$	\bigodot
$\bigoplus$	\bigoplus	$\bigotimes$	\bigotimes		

Table 3.6: Arrows.

$\leftarrow$	\leftarrow or \gets	$\longleftarrow$	\longleftarrow
$\rightarrow$	\rightarrow or \to	$\longrightarrow$	\longrightarrow
$\leftrightarrow$	\leftrightarrow	$\longleftrightarrow$	\longleftrightarrow
$\Leftarrow$	\Leftarrow	$\Longleftarrow$	\Longleftarrow
$\Rightarrow$	\Rightarrow	$\Longrightarrow$	\Longrightarrow
$\Leftrightarrow$	\Leftrightarrow	$\Longleftrightarrow$	\Longleftrightarrow
$\mapsto$	\mapsto	$\longmapsto$	\longmapsto
$\hookleftarrow$	\hookleftarrow	$\hookrightarrow$	\hookrightarrow
$\leftharpoonup$	\leftharpoonup	$\rightharpoonup$	\rightharpoonup
$\leftharpoondown$	\leftharpoondown	$\rightharpoondown$	\rightharpoondown
$\rightleftharpoons$	\rightleftharpoons	$\Longleftrightarrow$	\iff (bigger spaces)
$\uparrow$	\uparrow	$\downarrow$	\downarrow
$\updownarrow$	\updownarrow	$\Uparrow$	\Uparrow
$\Downarrow$	\Downarrow	$\Updownarrow$	\Updownarrow
$\nearrow$	\nearrow	$\searrow$	\searrow
$\swarrow$	\swarrow	$\nwarrow$	\nwarrow
$\leadsto$	\leadsto [a]		

[a]Use the latexsym package to access this symbol

Table 3.7: Arrows as Accents.

$\overrightarrow{AB}$	\overrightarrow{AB}	$\underrightarrow{AB}$	\underrightarrow{AB}
$\overleftarrow{AB}$	\overleftarrow{AB}	$\underleftarrow{AB}$	\underleftarrow{AB}
$\overleftrightarrow{AB}$	\overleftrightarrow{AB}	$\underleftrightarrow{AB}$	\underleftrightarrow{AB}

Table 3.8: Delimiters.

(	(	)	)	↑	\uparrow
[	[or \lbrack	]	] or \rbrack	↓	\downarrow
{	\{ or \lbrace	}	\} or \rbrace	↕	\updownarrow
⟨	\langle	⟩	\rangle	⇑	\Uparrow
|	| or \vert	‖	\\| or \Vert	⇓	\Downarrow
/	/	\	\backslash	⇕	\Updownarrow
⌊	\lfloor	⌋	\rfloor		
⌉	\rceil	⌈	\lceil		

Table 3.9: Large Delimiters.

⎛	\lgroup	⎞	\rgroup	⎰	\lmoustache
⏐	\arrowvert	‖	\Arrowvert	⎢	\bracevert
⎝	\rmoustache				

Table 3.10: Miscellaneous Symbols.

...	\dots	⋯	\cdots	⋮	\vdots	⋰	\ddots
$\hbar$	\hbar	$\imath$	\imath	$\jmath$	\jmath	ℓ	\ell
$\Re$	\Re	$\Im$	\Im	$\aleph$	\aleph	$\wp$	\wp
$\forall$	\forall	$\exists$	\exists	$\mho$	\mho [a]	∂	\partial
$'$	,	$\prime$	\prime	$\emptyset$	\emptyset	∞	\infty
∇	\nabla	$\triangle$	\triangle	$\Box$	\Box [a]	$\Diamond$	\Diamond [a]
$\bot$	\bot	$\top$	\top	$\angle$	\angle	$\surd$	\surd
$\diamondsuit$	\diamondsuit	$\heartsuit$	\heartsuit	♣	\clubsuit	♠	\spadesuit
$\neg$	\neg or \lnot	$\flat$	\flat	$\natural$	\natural	$\sharp$	\sharp

[a]Use the latexsym package to access this symbol

Table 3.11: Non-Mathematical Symbols.

These symbols can also be used in text mode.

†	\dag	§	\S	©	\copyright	®	\textregistered
‡	\ddag	¶	\P	£	\pounds	%	\%

Table 3.12: $\mathcal{AMS}$ Delimiters.

⌈	\ulcorner	⌉	\urcorner	⌊	\llcorner	⌋	\lrcorner
		\lvert			\rvert	‖	\lVert	‖	\rVert

Table 3.13: $\mathcal{AMS}$ Greek and Hebrew.

ϝ	\digamma	ϰ	\varkappa	ℶ	\beth	ℷ	\gimel	ℸ	\daleth

Table 3.14: Math Alphabets.

See Table 6.4 on 125 for other math fonts.

Example	Command	Required package
ABCDEabcde1234	\mathrm{ABCDE abcde 1234}	
ABCDEabcde1234	\mathit{ABCDE abcde 1234}	
*ABCDEabcde*1234	\mathnormal{ABCDE abcde 1234}	
$\mathcal{ABCDE}$	\mathcal{ABCDE abcde 1234}	
$\mathscr{ABCDE}$	\mathscr{ABCDE abcde 1234}	mathrsfs
$\mathfrak{ABCDE}$abcde1234	\mathfrak{ABCDE abcde 1234}	amsfonts or amssymb
$\mathbb{ABCDE}$	\mathbb{ABCDE abcde 1234}	amsfonts or amssymb

Table 3.15: $\mathcal{AMS}$ Binary Operators.

∔	\dotplus	⋅	\centerdot		
⋉	\ltimes	⋊	\rtimes	⋇	\divideontimes
⋓	\doublecup	⋒	\doublecap	∖	\smallsetminus
⊻	\veebar	⊼	\barwedge	⩞	\doublebarwedge
⊞	\boxplus	⊟	\boxminus	⊝	\circleddash
⊠	\boxtimes	⊡	\boxdot	⊚	\circledcirc
⊺	\intercal	⊛	\circledast	⋋	\rightthreetimes
⋎	\curlyvee	⋏	\curlywedge	⋌	\leftthreetimes

Table 3.16: $\mathcal{AMS}$ Binary Relations.

⋖	\lessdot	⋗	\gtrdot	≐	\doteqdot
⩽	\leqslant	⩾	\geqslant	≓	\risingdotseq
⪕	\eqslantless	⪖	\eqslantgtr	≒	\fallingdotseq
≦	\leqq	≧	\geqq	≖	\eqcirc
⋘	\lll or \llless	⋙	\ggg	≗	\circeq
≲	\lesssim	≳	\gtrsim	≜	\triangleq
⪅	\lessapprox	⪆	\gtrapprox	≏	\bumpeq
≶	\lessgtr	≷	\gtrless	≎	\Bumpeq
⋚	\lesseqgtr	⋛	\gtreqless	∼	\thicksim
⪋	\lesseqqgtr	⪌	\gtreqqless	≈	\thickapprox
≼	\preccurlyeq	≽	\succcurlyeq	≊	\approxeq
⋞	\curlyeqprec	⋟	\curlyeqsucc	∽	\backsim
≾	\precsim	≿	\succsim	⋍	\backsimeq
⪷	\precapprox	⪸	\succapprox	⊨	\vDash
⊆	\subseteqq	⊇	\supseteqq	⊩	\Vdash
∥	\shortparallel	⋑	\Supset	⊪	\Vvdash
◄	\blacktriangleleft	⊐	\sqsupset	϶	\backepsilon
▷	\vartriangleright	∵	\because	∝	\varpropto
►	\blacktriangleright	⋐	\Subset	≬	\between
⊵	\trianglerighteq	⌢	\smallfrown	⋔	\pitchfork
◁	\vartriangleleft	∣	\shortmid	⌣	\smallsmile
⊴	\trianglelefteq	∴	\therefore	⊏	\sqsubset

Table 3.17: $\mathcal{AMS}$ Arrows.

←--	\dashleftarrow	--→	\dashrightarrow
⇇	\leftleftarrows	⇉	\rightrightarrows
⇆	\leftrightarrows	⇄	\rightleftarrows
⇚	\Lleftarrow	⇛	\Rrightarrow
↞	\twoheadleftarrow	↠	\twoheadrightarrow
↢	\leftarrowtail	↣	\rightarrowtail
⇋	\leftrightharpoons	⇌	\rightleftharpoons
↰	\Lsh	↱	\Rsh
↩	\looparrowleft	↪	\looparrowright
↶	\curvearrowleft	↷	\curvearrowright
↺	\circlearrowleft	↻	\circlearrowright
⊸	\multimap	⇈	\upuparrows
⇊	\downdownarrows	↿	\upharpoonleft
↾	\upharpoonright	⇂	\downharpoonright
⇝	\rightsquigarrow	↭	\leftrightsquigarrow

Table 3.18: $\mathcal{AMS}$ Negated Binary Relations and Arrows.

≮	\nless	≯	\ngtr	⊊	\varsubsetneqq
≨	\lneq	≩	\gneq	⊋	\varsupsetneqq
≰	\nleq	≱	\ngeq	⊈	\nsubseteqq
≰	\nleqslant	≱	\ngeqslant	⊉	\nsupseteqq
≨	\lneqq	≩	\gneqq	∤	\nmid
≨	\lvertneqq	≩	\gvertneqq	∦	\nparallel
≨	\nleqq	≩	\ngeqq	∤	\nshortmid
⋦	\lnsim	⋧	\gnsim	∦	\nshortparallel
⪉	\lnapprox	⪊	\gnapprox	≁	\nsim
⊀	\nprec	⊁	\nsucc	≇	\ncong
⋠	\npreceq	⋡	\nsucceq	⊬	\nvdash
⪵	\precneqq	⪶	\succneqq	⊭	\nvDash
⋨	\precnsim	⋩	\succnsim	⊮	\nVdash
⪹	\precnapprox	⪺	\succnapprox	⊯	\nVDash
⊊	\subsetneq	⊋	\supsetneq	⋪	\ntriangleleft
⊊	\varsubsetneq	⊋	\varsupsetneq	⋫	\ntriangleright
⊄	\nsubseteq	⊅	\nsupseteq	⋬	\ntrianglelefteq
⊊	\subsetneqq	⊋	\supsetneqq	⋭	\ntrianglerighteq
↚	\nleftarrow	↛	\nrightarrow	↮	\nleftrightarrow
⇍	\nLeftarrow	⇏	\nRightarrow	⇎	\nLeftrightarrow

Table 3.19: $\mathcal{AMS}$ Miscellaneous.

ℏ	\hbar	ℏ	\hslash	⫿	\Bbbk
□	\square	■	\blacksquare	Ⓢ	\circledS
△	\vartriangle	▲	\blacktriangle	∁	\complement
▽	\triangledown	▼	\blacktriangledown	⅁	\Game
◇	\lozenge	◆	\blacklozenge	★	\bigstar
∠	\angle	∡	\measuredangle		
╱	\diagup	╲	\diagdown	‵	\backprime
∄	\nexists	⅂	\Finv	∅	\varnothing
ð	\eth	∢	\sphericalangle	℧	\mho

Chapter 4

Specialities

When putting together a large document, LaTeX will help with some special features like index generation, bibliography management, and other things. A much more complete description of specialities and enhancements possible with LaTeX can be found in the *LaTeX Manual* [1] and *The LaTeX Companion* [3].

4.1 Including Encapsulated PostScript

LaTeX provides the basic facilities to work with floating bodies, such as images or graphics, with the `figure` and `table` environments.

There are several ways to generate the actual graphics with basic LaTeX or a LaTeX extension package, a few of them are described in chapter 5. Please refer to *The LaTeX Companion* [3] and the *LaTeX Manual* [1] for more information on that subject.

A much easier way to get graphics into a document is to generate them with a specialised software package[1] and then include the finished graphics in the document. Here again, LaTeX packages offer many ways to do this, but this introduction will only discuss the use of Encapsulated POSTSCRIPT (EPS) graphics, because it is quite easy to do and widely used. In order to use pictures in the EPS format, you must have a POSTSCRIPT printer[2] available for output.

A good set of commands for inclusion of graphics is provided in the graphicx package by D. P. Carlisle. It is part of a whole family of packages called the "graphics" bundle.[3]

When working on a system with a POSTSCRIPT printer available for output and with the graphicx package installed, use the following step by

---

[1]Such as XFig, Gnuplot, Gimp, Xara X . . .

[2]Another possibility to output POSTSCRIPT is the GHOSTSCRIPT program available from `CTAN://support/ghostscript`. Windows and OS/2 users might want to look for GSVIEW.

[3]`CTAN://pkg/graphics`

step guide to include a picture into your document:

1. Export the picture from your graphics program in EPS format.[4]

2. Load the graphicx package in the preamble of the input file with

    ```
    \usepackage[driver]{graphicx}
    ```

    where *driver* is the name of your "dvi to POSTSCRIPT" converter program. The most widely used program is called dvips. The name of the driver is required, because there is no standard on how graphics are included in TEX. Knowing the name of the *driver*, the graphicx package can choose the correct method to insert information about the graphics into the .dvi file, so that the printer understands it and can correctly include the .eps file.

3. Use the command

    ```
    \includegraphics[key=value, ...]{file}
    ```

    to include *file* into your document. The optional parameter accepts a comma separated list of *keys* and associated *values*. The *keys* can be used to alter the width, height and rotation of the included graphic. Table 4.1 lists the most important keys.

Table 4.1: Key Names for graphicx Package.

width	scale graphic to the specified width
height	scale graphic to the specified height
angle	rotate graphic counterclockwise
scale	scale graphic

---

[4]If your software cannot export into EPS format, you can try to install a POSTSCRIPT printer driver (such as an Apple LaserWriter, for example) and then print to a file with this driver. With some luck this file will be in EPS format. Note that an EPS must not contain more than one page. Some printer drivers can be explicitly configured to produce EPS format.

The following example code may help to clarify things:

```
\begin{figure}
\centering
\includegraphics[angle=90,
                 width=0.5\textwidth]{test}
\caption{This is a test.}
\end{figure}
```

It includes the graphic stored in the file `test.eps`. The graphic is *first* rotated by an angle of 90 degrees and *then* scaled to the final width of 0.5 times the width of a standard paragraph. The aspect ratio is 1.0, because no special height is specified. The width and height parameters can also be specified in absolute dimensions. Refer to Table 6.5 on page 130 for more information. If you want to know more about this topic, make sure to read [9] and [13].

4.2 Bibliography

Produce a bibliography with the `thebibliography` environment. Each entry starts with

```
\bibitem[label]{marker}
```

The *marker* is then used to cite the book, article or paper within the document.

```
\cite{marker}
```

If you do not use the *label* option, the entries will get enumerated automatically. The parameter after the `\begin{thebibliography}` command defines how much space to reserve for the number of labels. In the example below, `{99}` tells LaTeX to expect that none of the bibliography item numbers will be wider than the number 99.

```
Partl~\cite{pa} has
proposed that \ldots
\begin{thebibliography}{99}
\bibitem{pa} H.~Partl:
\emph{German \TeX},
TUGboat Volume~9, Issue~1 (1988)
\end{thebibliography}
```

Partl [1] has proposed that ...

Bibliography

[1] H. Partl: *German TeX*, TUGboat Volume 9, Issue 1 (1988)

For larger projects, you might want to check out the BibTeX program. BibTeX is included with most TeX distributions. It allows you to maintain a bibliographic database and then extract the references relevant to things you cited in your paper. The visual presentation of BibTeX-generated bibliographies is based on a style-sheets concept that allows you to create bibliographies following a wide range of established designs.

4.3 Indexing

A very useful feature of many books is their index. With LaTeX and the support program `makeindex`,[5] an index can be generated quite easily. This introduction will only explain the basic index generation commands. For a more in-depth view, please refer to *The LaTeX Companion* [3].

To enable their indexing feature of LaTeX, the `makeidx` package must be loaded in the preamble with

```
\usepackage{makeidx}
```

and the special indexing commands must be enabled by putting the

```
\makeindex
```

command in the preamble.

The content of the index is specified with

```
\index{key@formatted_entry}
```

commands, where *formatted_entry* will appear in the index and *key* will be used for sorting. The *formatted_entry* is optional. If it is missing the *key* will be used. You enter the index commands at the points in the text that you want the final index entries to point to. Table 4.2 explains the syntax with several examples.

When the input file is processed with LaTeX, each `\index` command writes an appropriate index entry, together with the current page number, to a special file. The file has the same name as the LaTeX input file, but a different extension (`.idx`). This `.idx` file can then be processed with the `makeindex` program:

```
makeindex filename
```

The `makeindex` program generates a sorted index with the same base file name, but this time with the extension `.ind`. If now the LaTeX input file is

---

[5]On systems not necessarily supporting filenames longer than 8 characters, the program may be called `makeidx`.

Table 4.2: Index Key Syntax Examples.

Example	Index Entry	Comment
\index{hello}	hello, 1	Plain entry
\index{hello!Peter}	Peter, 3	Subentry under 'hello'
\index{Sam@\textsl{Sam}}	*Sam*, 2	Formatted entry
\index{Lin@\textbf{Lin}}	**Lin**, 7	Formatted entry
\index{Kaese@K\"ase}	**Käse**, 33	Formatted entry
\index{ecole@\'ecole}	école, 4	Formatted entry
\index{Jenny|textbf}	Jenny, **3**	Formatted page number
\index{Joe|textit}	Joe, *5*	Formatted page number

processed again, this sorted index gets included into the document at the point where LATEX finds

```
\printindex
```

The showidx package that comes with LATEX 2_ε prints out all index entries in the left margin of the text. This is quite useful for proofreading a document and verifying the index.

Note that the \index command can affect your layout if not used carefully.

```
My Word \index{Word}. As opposed
to Word\index{Word}. Note the
position of the full stop.
```

> My Word . As opposed to Word. Note the position of the full stop.

makeindex has no clue about characters outside the ASCII range. To get the sorting correct, use the @ character as shown in the Käse and école examples above.

4.4 Fancy Headers

The fancyhdr package,[6] written by Piet van Oostrum, provides a few simple commands that allow you to customize the header and footer lines of your document. Look at the top of this page, for an application of this package.

The tricky problem when customising headers and footers is to get things like running section and chapter names in there. LATEX accomplishes this with a two-stage approach. In the header and footer definition, you use the commands \rightmark and \leftmark to represent the current section

---

[6]Available from CTAN://macros/latex/contrib/supported/fancyhdr.

```
\documentclass{book}
\usepackage{fancyhdr}
\pagestyle{fancy}
% with this we ensure that the chapter and section
% headings are in lowercase.
\renewcommand{\chaptermark}[1]{%
        \markboth{#1}{}}
\renewcommand{\sectionmark}[1]{%
        \markright{\thesection\ #1}}
\fancyhf{}  % delete current header and footer
\fancyhead[LE,RO]{\bfseries\thepage}
\fancyhead[LO]{\bfseries\rightmark}
\fancyhead[RE]{\bfseries\leftmark}
\renewcommand{\headrulewidth}{0.5pt}
\renewcommand{\footrulewidth}{0pt}
\addtolength{\headheight}{0.5pt} % space for the rule
\fancypagestyle{plain}{%
    \fancyhead{} % get rid of headers on plain pages
    \renewcommand{\headrulewidth}{0pt} % and the line
}
```

Figure 4.1: Example fancyhdr Setup.

and chapter heading, respectively. The values of these two commands are overwritten whenever a chapter or section command is processed.

For ultimate flexibility, the \chapter command and its friends do not redefine \rightmark and \leftmark themselves. They call yet another command (\chaptermark, \sectionmark, or \subsectionmark) that is responsible for redefining \rightmark and \leftmark.

If you want to change the look of the chapter name in the header line, you need only "renew" the \chaptermark command.

Figure 4.1 shows a possible setup for the fancyhdr package that makes the headers look about the same as they look in this booklet. In any case, I suggest you fetch the documentation for the package at the address mentioned in the footnote.

4.5   The Verbatim Package

Earlier in this book, you got to know the verbatim *environment*. In this section, you are going to learn about the verbatim *package*. The verbatim package is basically a re-implementation of the verbatim environment that works around some of the limitations of the original verbatim environment. This by itself is not spectacular, but the implementation of the verbatim package added new functionality, which is why I am mentioning the package here. The verbatim package provides the

> \verbatiminput{*filename*}

command, which allows you to include raw ASCII text into your document as if it were inside a verbatim environment.

As the verbatim package is part of the 'tools' bundle, you should find it pre-installed on most systems. If you want to know more about this package, make sure to read [10].

4.6   Installing Extra Packages

Most LaTeX installations come with a large set of pre-installed style packages, but many more are available on the net. The main place to look for style packages on the Internet is CTAN (http://www.ctan.org/).

Packages such as geometry, hyphenat, and many others are typically made up of two files: a file with the extension .ins and another with the extension .dtx. There will often be a readme.txt with a brief description of the package. You should of course read this file first.

In any event, once you have copied the package files onto your machine, you still have to process them in a way that (a) tells your TeX distribution about the new style package and (b) gives you the documentation. Here's how you do the first part:

1. Run LaTeX on the `.ins` file. This will extract a `.sty` file.

2. Move the `.sty` file to a place where your distribution can find it. Usually this is in your `.../localtexmf/tex/latex` subdirectory (Windows or OS/2 users should feel free to change the direction of the slashes).

3. Refresh your distribution's file-name database. The command depends on the LaTeX distribution you use: TeXlive – `texhash`; web2c – `maktexlsr`; MiKTeX – `initexmf --update-fndb` or use the GUI.

Now extract the documentation from the `.dtx` file:

1. Run LaTeX on the `.dtx` file. This will generate a `.dvi` file. Note that you may have to run LaTeX several times before it gets the cross-references right.

2. Check to see if LaTeX has produced a `.idx` file among the various files you now have. If you do not see this file, then the documentation has no index. Continue with step 5.

3. In order to generate the index, type the following:
   ```
   makeindex -s gind.ist name
   ```
   (where *name* stands for the main-file name without any extension).

4. Run LaTeX on the `.dtx` file once again.

5. Last but not least, make a `.ps` or `.pdf` file to increase your reading pleasure.

Sometimes you will see that a `.glo` (glossary) file has been produced. Run the following command between step 4 and 5:
```
makeindex -s gglo.ist -o name.gls name.glo
```
Be sure to run LaTeX on the `.dtx` one last time before moving on to step 5.

4.7 Working with pdfLaTeX

By Daniel Flipo <Daniel.Flipo@univ-lille1.fr>

PDF is a portable hypertext document format. Much as in a web page, some words in the document are marked as hyperlinks. They link to other places in the document or even to other documents. If you click on such a hyperlink you get transported to the destination of the link. In the context of LaTeX, this means that all occurrences of `\ref` and `\pageref` become hyperlinks. Additionally, the table of contents, the index and all the other similar structures become collections of hyperlinks.

Most web pages you find today are written in HTML *(HyperText Markup Language)*. This format has two significant disadvantages when writing scientific documents:

1. Including mathematical formulae into HTML documents is not generally supported. While there is a standard for it, most browsers used today do not support it, or lack the required fonts.

2. Printing HTML documents is possible, but the results vary widely between platforms and browsers. The results are miles removed from the quality we have come to expect in the LATEX world.

There have been many attempts to create translators from LATEX to HTML. Some were even quite successful in the sense that they are able to produce legible web pages from a standard LATEX input file. But all of them cut corners left and right to get the job done. As soon as you start using more complex LATEX features and external packages things tend to fall apart. Authors wishing to preserve the unique typographic quality of their documents even when publishing on the web turn to PDF *(Portable Document Format)*, which preserves the layout of the document and permits hypertext navigation. Most modern browsers come with plugins that allow the direct display of PDF documents.

Even though there are DVI and PS viewers for almost every platform, you will find that Acrobat Reader and Xpdf for viewing PDF documents are more widely deployed[7]. So providing PDF versions of your documents will make them much more accessible to your potential readers.

4.7.1   PDF Documents for the Web

The creation of a PDF file from LATEX source is very simple, thanks to the pdfTEX program developed by Hàn Thế Thành. pdfTEX produces PDF output where normal TEX produces DVI. There is also a pdfLATEX, which produces PDF output from LATEX sources.

Both pdfTEX and pdfLATEX are installed automatically by most modern TEX distributions, such as teTEX, fpTEX, MikTEX, TEXLive and CMacTEX.

To produce a PDF instead of DVI, it is sufficient to replace the command `latex file.tex` by `pdflatex file.tex`. On systems where LATEX is not called from the command line, you may find a special button in the TEX GUI.

Set the paper size with an optional documentclass argument such as `a4paper` or `letterpaper`. This works in pdfLATEX too, but on top of this pdfTEX also needs to know the physical size of the paper to determine the physical size of the pages in the pdf file. If you use the hyperref package (see page 93), the papersize will be adjusted automatically. Otherwise you have

---

[7]http://pdfreaders.org

to do this manually by putting the following lines into the preamble of the document:

```
\pdfpagewidth=\paperwidth
\pdfpageheight=\paperheight
```

The following section will go into more detail regarding the differences between normal LaTeX and pdfLaTeX. The main differences concern three areas: the fonts to use, the format of images to include, and the manual configuration of hyperlinks.

4.7.2   The Fonts

pdfLaTeX can deal with all sorts of fonts (PK bitmaps, TrueType, POSTSCRIPT type 1...) but the normal LaTeX font format, the bitmap PK fonts produce very ugly results when the document is displayed with Acrobat Reader. It is best to use POSTSCRIPT Type 1 fonts exclusively to produce documents that display well. *Modern TeX installations will be set up so that this happens automatically. Best is to try. If it works for you, just skip this whole section.*

The Type 1 font set most widely used today is called Latin Modern (LM). If you have a recent TeX installation, chances are that you already have a copy of them installed; all you need to do is to add

```
\usepackage{lmodern}
\usepackage[T1]{fontenc}
\usepackage{textcomp}
```

to the preamble of your document and you are all set for creating excellent PDF output with full support for the full Latin character set. If you are working with a stripped down setup, you may have to add the lm fonts explicitly.

For the Russian language you may want to use C1 virtual fonts, available at `ftp://ftp.vsu.ru/pub/tex/font-packs/c1fonts`. These fonts combine the standard CM type 1 fonts from Bluesky collection and CMCYR type 1 fonts from the Paradissa and BaKoMa collection, all available on CTAN. Because Paradissa fonts contain only Russian letters, C1 fonts are missing other Cyrillic glyphs.

Another solution is to switch to other POSTSCRIPT type 1 fonts. Actually, some of them are even included with every copy of Acrobat Reader. Because these fonts have different character sizes, the text layout on your pages will change. Generally these other fonts will use more space than the CM fonts, which are very space-efficient. Also, the overall visual coherence of your document will suffer because Times, Helvetica and Courier (the primary candidates for such a replacement job) have not been designed to work in harmony in a single document.

Two ready-made font sets are available for this purpose: pxfonts, which is based on *Palatino* as its main text body font, and the txfonts package, which is based on *Times*. To use them it is sufficient to put the following lines into the preamble of your document:

```
\usepackage[T1]{fontenc}
\usepackage{pxfonts}
```

You may find lines like

```
Warning: pdftex (file eurmo10): Font eur... not found
```

in the .log file after compiling your input file. They mean that some font used in the document has not been found. Make sure you identify and fix the offending parts of your document, as the resulting PDF document may *not display the pages with the missing characters at all*.

4.7.3   Using Graphics

Including graphics into a document works best with the graphicx package (see page 83):

```
\usepackage{xcolor,graphicx}
```

In the sample above I have included the color package, as using color in documents displayed on the web comes quite naturally.

So much for the good news. The bad news is that graphics in Encapsulated POSTSCRIPT format do not work with pdfLaTeX. If you don't define a file extension in the \includegraphics command, graphicx will go looking for a suitable file on its own, depending on the setting of the *driver* option. For pdftex this is formats .png, .pdf, .jpg and .mps (METAPOST)—but *not* .eps.

The simple way out of this problem is to just convert your EPS files into PDF format using the epstopdf utility found on many systems. For vector graphics (drawings) this is a great solution. For bitmaps (photos, scans) this is not ideal, because the PDF format natively supports the inclusion of PNG and JPEG images. PNG is good for screenshots and other images with few colours. JPEG is great for photos, as it is very space-efficient.

It may even be desirable not to draw certain geometric figures, but rather describe the figure with a specialized command language, such as META-POST, which can be found in most TeX distributions, and comes with its own extensive manual.

4.7.4   Hypertext Links

The hyperref package will take care of turning all internal references of your document into hyperlinks. For this to work properly some magic is necessary, so you have to put `\usepackage[pdftex]{hyperref}` as the *last* command into the preamble of your document.

Many options are available to customize the behaviour of the hyperref package:

- either as a comma separated list after the pdftex option
  `\usepackage[pdftex]{hyperref}`

- or on individual lines with the command `\hypersetup{`*options*`}`.

The only required option is `pdftex`; the others are optional and allow you to change the default behaviour of hyperref.[8] In the following list the default values are written in an upright font.

bookmarks (=true,*false*) show or hide the bookmarks bar when displaying the document

unicode (=false,*true*) allows the use of characters of non-latin based languages in Acrobat's bookmarks

pdftoolbar (=true,*false*) show or hide Acrobat's toolbar

pdfmenubar (=true,*false*) show or hide Acrobat's menu

pdffitwindow (=false,*true*) adjust the initial magnification of the PDF when displayed

pdftitle (={text}) define the title that gets displayed in the Document Info window of Acrobat

pdfauthor (={text}) the name of the PDF's author

pdfnewwindow (=false,*true*) define whether a new window should be opened when a link leads out of the current document

colorlinks (=false,*true*) surround the links by colour frames (false) or colour the text of the links (true). The colour of these links can be configured using the following options (default colours are shown):

linkcolor (=red) colour of internal links (sections, pages, etc.)

citecolor (=green) colour of citation links (bibliography)

filecolor (=magenta) colour of file links

urlcolor (=cyan) colour of URL links (mail, web)

---

[8]It is worth noting that the hyperref package is not limited to work with pdfTeX. It can also be configured to embed PDF-specific information into the DVI output of normal LaTeX, which then gets put into the PS file by `dvips` and is finally picked up by the pdf convertor when turning the PS file into PDF.

If you are happy with the defaults, use

```
\usepackage[pdftex]{hyperref}
```

To have the bookmark list open and links in colour (the =true values are optional):

```
\usepackage[pdftex,bookmarks,colorlinks]{hyperref}
```

When creating PDFs destined for printing, coloured links are not a good thing as they end up in gray in the final output, making it difficult to read. Use colour frames, which are not printed:

```
\usepackage{hyperref}
\hypersetup{colorlinks=false}
```

or make links black:

```
\usepackage{hyperref}
\hypersetup{colorlinks,%
            citecolor=black,%
            filecolor=black,%
            linkcolor=black,%
            urlcolor=black,%
            pdftex}
```

When you just want to provide information for the Document Info section of the PDF file:

```
\usepackage[pdfauthor={Pierre Desproges},%
            pdftitle={Des femmes qui tombent},%
            pdftex]{hyperref}
```

In addition to the automatic hyperlinks for cross references, it is possible to embed explicit links using

---

`\href{url}{text}`

The code

```
The \href{http://www.ctan.org}{CTAN} website.
```

produces the output "CTAN"; a click on the word "CTAN" will take you to the CTAN website.

If the destination of the link is not a URL but a local file, use the \href command without the 'http://' bit:

```
The complete document is \href{manual.pdf}{here}
```

which produces the text "The complete document is here". A click on the word "here" will open the file `manual.pdf`. (The filename is relative to the location of the current document).

The author of an article might want her readers to easily send email messages by using the `\href` command inside the `\author` command on the title page of the document:

```
\author{Mary Oetiker $<$\href{mailto:mary@oetiker.ch}%
        {mary@oetiker.ch}$>$
```

Note that I have put the link so that my email address appears not only in the link but also on the page itself. I did this because the link
`\href{mailto:mary@oetiker.ch}{Mary Oetiker}`
would work well within Acrobat, but once the page is printed the email address would not be visible anymore.

4.7.5   Problems with Links

Messages like the following:

```
! pdfTeX warning (ext4): destination with the same
  identifier (name{page.1}) has been already used,
  duplicate ignored
```

appear when a counter gets reinitialized, for example by using the command `\mainmatter` provided by the `book` document class. It resets the page number counter to 1 prior to the first chapter of the book. But as the preface of the book also has a page number 1 all links to "page 1" would not be unique anymore, hence the notice that "`duplicate` has been `ignored`."

The counter measure consists of putting `plainpages=false` into the hyperref options. This unfortunately only helps with the page counter. An even more radical solution is to use the option
`hypertexnames=false`, but this will cause the page links in the index to stop working.

4.7.6   Problems with Bookmarks

The text displayed by bookmarks does not always look like you expect it to look. Because bookmarks are "just text," fewer characters are available for bookmarks than for normal LaTeX text. Hyperref will normally notice such problems and put up a warning:

```
Package hyperref Warning:
Token not allowed in a PDFDocEncoded string:
```

Work around this problem by providing a text string for the bookmarks, which replaces the offending text:

> \texorpdfstring{*TEX text*}{*Bookmark Text*}

Math expressions are a prime candidate for this kind of problem:

```
\section{\texorpdfstring{$E=mc^2$}%
        {E = mc ** 2}}
```

which turns `\section{$E=mc^2$}` to "E = mc ** 2" in the bookmark area.

If you write your document in Unicode and use the `unicode` option for the hyperref package to use Unicode characters in bookmarks, this will give you a much larger selection of characters to pick from when when using `\texorpdfstring`.

4.7.7 Source Compatibility Between LaTeX and pdfLaTeX

Ideally your document would compile equally well with LaTeX and pdfLaTeX. The main problem in this respect is the inclusion of graphics. The simple solution is to *systematically drop* the file extension from `\includegraphics` commands. They will then automatically look for a file of a suitable format in the current directory. All you have to do is create appropriate versions of the graphics files. LaTeX will look for `.eps`, and pdfLaTeX will try to include a file with the extension `.png`, `.pdf`, `.jpg` or `.mps` (in that order).

For the cases where you want to use different code for the PDF version of your document, simply add the package ifpdf[9] to your preamble. Chances are that you already have it installed; if not then you're probably using MiKTeX which will install it for you automatically the first time you try to use it. This package defines the special command `\ifpdf` that will allow you to write conditional code easily. In this example, we want the POSTSCRIPT version to be black and white due to the printing costs but we want the PDF version for online viewing to be colourful.

```
\RequirePackage{ifpdf} % are we producing PDF ?
\documentclass[a4paper,12pt]{book}
\usepackage[latin1]{inputenc}
\usepackage[T1]{fontenc}
\usepackage{lmodern}
\usepackage[bookmarks, % tune hyperref
           colorlinks,
           plainpages=false]{hyperref}
\usepackage{graphicx}
```

---

[9] If you want the whole story on why to use this package then go to the TEX FAQ under the item http://www.tex.ac.uk/cgi-bin/texfaq2html?label=ifpdf.

```
\ifpdf
  \hypersetup{linkscolor=blue}
\else
  \hypersetup{linkscolors=black}
\fi
\usepackage[english]{babel}
  ...
```

In the example above I have included the hyperref package even in the non-PDF version. The effect of this is to make the \href command work in all cases, which saves me from wrapping every occurrence into a conditional statement.

Note that in recent TEX distributions (like TEXLive, MacTEX and MiKTEX), the normal TEX program is actually pdfTEX and it will automatically switch between producing pdf and dvi according to the name it is called with: use the pdflatex command to get pdf output and latex for normal dvi output.

4.8 Working with X∃LATEX

By Axel Kielhorn <A.Kielhorn@web.de>

Most of the things said about pdfLATEX are valid for X∃LATEX as well.

There is a Wiki at http://wiki.xelatex.org/doku.php that collects information relevant to X∃TEX and X∃LATEX.

4.8.1 The Fonts

In addition to the normal tfm based fonts, X∃LATEX is able to use any font known to the operating system. If you have the Linux Libertine fonts installed, you can simply say

```
\usepackage{fontspec}
\setmainfont[Ligatures=TeX]{Linux Libertine}
```

in the preamble. This will normally detect the italic and bold versions as well, so \textit and \textbf will work as usual. When the font is using OpenType technology you have access to many features which required switching to a separate font or using virtual fonts in the past. The main feature is the extended character set; a font may contain Latin, Greek and Cyrillic characters and the corresponding ligatures.

Many fonts contain at least two kinds of numerals, the normal lining numerals and so called old style (or lower case) numerals, which partly extend below the baseline. They may contain proportional numerals (the "1" takes less space than the "0") or monospaced numerals which are suitable for tables.

```
\newfontfamily\LLln[Numbers=Lining]{(font)}
\newfontfamily\LLos[Numbers=OldStyle]{(font)}
\newfontfamily\LLlnm[Numbers=Lining,Numbers=Monospaced]{(font)}
\newfontfamily\LLosm[Numbers=OldStyle,Numbers=Monospaced]{(font)}
```

Almost all OpenType fonts contain the standard ligatures (fl fi ffi) but there are also some rare or historical ligatures like st, ct and tz. You may not want to use them in a technical report but they are fine for a novel. To enable these ligatures use either of the following lines:

```
\setmainfont[Ligatures=Rare]{(font)}
\setmainfont[Ligatures=Historic]{(font)}
\setmainfont[Ligatures=Historic,Ligatures=Rare]{(font)}
```

Not every font contains both sets of ligature, consult the font documentation or just try it out. Sometimes these ligatures are language dependent; for example a ligature used in Polish (fk) is not used in English. You have to add

```
\setmainfont[Language=Polish]{(font)}
```

to enable the Polish ligatures.

Some fonts (like the commercial Adobe Garamond Premier Pro) contain alternative glyphs that are activated by default in X‑LATEX distributed with TEXLive 2010[10]. The result is a stylish "Q" with a descender reaching below the following "u". To disable this feature you have to define the font with disabled contextuals:

```
\setmainfont[Contextuals=NoAlternate]{(font)}
```

To learn about fonts in X‑LATEX read the fontspec manual.

Where do I get OpenType fonts?

If you have TeXLive installed, you already have some at .../texmf-dist/fonts/opentype, just install them in your operating system. This collection does not include DejaVu, which is available at http://dejavu-fonts.org/.

Make sure that each font is only installed *once*, otherwise interesting results may happen.

You can use every font installed on your computer, but remember that other users may not have these fonts. The Zapfino font used in the fontspec manual is included in Mac OSX, but is not available on Windows computers.[11]

---

[10]The behavior has changed with this version, it was off by default in earlier releases.

[11]A commercial version of the font called Zapfino Extra is available.

Entering Unicode Characters

The number of characters in a font has grown but the number of keys on a regular keyboard has not. So, how do I enter non-ASCII characters?

If you write a large amount of text in a foreign language, you can install a keyboard for that language and print out the character positions. (Most operatings system have some sort of virtual keyboard, just make a screenshot.)

If you rarely need an exotic character, you can simply pick it in the character palette.

Some environments (e. g. the X Window System) offer many methods to enter non-ASCII characters. Some editors (e. g. Vim and Emacs) offer ways to enter these characters. Read the manual for the tools you are using.

4.8.2   Compatibility Between X⅁LATEX and pdfLATEX

There are a few things that are different between X⅁LATEX and pdfLATEX.

- A X⅁LATEX document has to be written in Unicode (UTF-8) while pdfLATEX may use different input encodings.

- The microtype packages does not work with X⅁LATEX yet, support for character protrusion is already under development.

- Everything font related has to be reviewed. (Unless you want to stick to Latin Modern.)

4.9   Creating Presentations

By Daniel Flipo <Daniel.Flipo@univ-lille1.fr>

You can present the results of your scientific work on a blackboard, with transparencies, or directly from your laptop using some presentation software.

pdfLATEX combined with the beamer class allows you to create presentations in PDF, looking much like something you might be able to generate with LibreOffice or PowerPoint if you had a very good day, but much more portable because PDF readers are available on many more systems.

The beamer class uses graphicx, color and hyperref with options adapted to screen presentations.

When you compile the code presented in figure 4.2 with pdfLATEX you get a PDF file with a title page and a second page showing several items that will be revealed one at a time as you step though your presentation.

One of the advantages of the beamer class is that it produces a PDF file that is directly usable without first going through a POSTSCRIPT stage like prosper or requiring additional post processing like presentations created with the ppower4 package.

```
\documentclass[10pt]{beamer}
\mode<beamer>{%
  \usetheme[hideothersubsections,
          right,width=22mm]{Goettingen}
}

\title{Simple Presentation}
\author[D. Flipo]{Daniel Flipo}
\institute{U.S.T.L. \& GUTenberg}
\titlegraphic{\includegraphics[width=20mm]{USTL}}
\date{2005}

\begin{document}

\begin{frame}<handout:0>
  \titlepage
\end{frame}

\section{An Example}

\begin{frame}
  \frametitle{Things to do on a Sunday Afternoon}
  \begin{block}{One could \ldots}
    \begin{itemize}
      \item walk the dog\dots \pause
      \item read a book\pause
      \item confuse a cat\pause
    \end{itemize}
  \end{block}
  and many other things
\end{frame}
\end{document}
```

Figure 4.2: Sample code for the beamer class

With the beamer class you can produce several versions (modes) of your document from the same input file. The input file may contain special instructions for the different modes in angular brackets. The following modes are available:

beamer for the presentation PDF discussed above.

trans for transparencies.

handout for the printed version.

The default mode is beamer, change it by setting a different mode as a global option, like \documentclass[10pt,handout]{beamer} to print the handouts for example.

The look of the screen presentation depends on the theme you choose. Pick one of the themes shipped with the beamer class or create your own. See the beamer class documentation in beameruserguide.pdf for more information on this.

Let's have a closer look at the code in figure 4.2.

For the screen version of the presentation \mode<beamer> we have chosen the *Goettingen* theme to show a navigation panel integrated into the table of contents. The options allow us to choose the size of the panel (22 mm in this case) and its position (on the right side of the body text). The option *hideothersubsections*, shows the chapter titles, but only the subsections of the present chapter. There are no special settings for \mode<trans> and \mode<handout>. They appear in their standard layout.

The commands \title{}, \author{}, \institute{}, and \titlegraphic{} set the content of the title page. The optional arguments of \title[]{} and \author[]{} let you specify a special version of the title and the author name to be displayed on the panel of the *Goettingen* theme.

The titles and subtitles in the panel are created with normal \section{} and \subsection{} commands that you place *outside* the frame environment.

The tiny navigation icons at the bottom of the screen also allow to navigate the document. Their presence is not dependent on the theme you choose.

The contents of each slide or screen has to be placed inside a frame environment. There is an optional argument in angular brackets (< and >), it allows us to suppress a particular frame in one of the versions of the presentation. In the example the first page would not be shown in the handout version due to the <handout:0> argument.

It is highly recommended to set a title for each slide apart from the title slide. This is done with the command \frametitle{}. If a subtitle is necessary use the block environment as shown in the example. Note that the sectioning commands \section{} and \subsection{} do not produce output on the slide proper.

The command `\pause` in the itemize environment lets you reveal the items one by one. For other presentation effects check out the commands `\only`, `\uncover`, `\alt` and `\temporal`. In many place it is possible to use angular brackets to further customize the presentation.

In any case make sure to read through the beamer class documentation `beameruserguide.pdf` to get a complete picture of what is in store for you. This package is being actively developed, check out their website to get the latest information. (http://latex-beamer.sourceforge.net/)

Chapter 5

Producing Mathematical Graphics

Most people use LaTeX for typesetting their text. And since the structure oriented approach to authoring is so convenient, LaTeX also offers a, if somewhat restricted, means for producing graphical output from textual descriptions. Furthermore, quite a number of LaTeX extensions have been created in order to overcome these restrictions. In this section, you will learn about a few of them.

5.1 Overview

Creating graphical output with LaTeX has a long tradition. It started out with the `picture` environment which allows you to create graphics by cleverly placing predefined elements onto the canvas. A complete description can be found in the *LaTeX Manual* [1]. The `picture` environment of LaTeX 2_ε brings with it the `\qbezier` command, "q" meaning "quadratic". Many frequently used curves such as circles, ellipses, or catenaries can be satisfactorily approximated by quadratic Bézier curves, although this may require some mathematical toil. If, in addition, a programming language is used to generate `\qbezier` blocks of LaTeX input files, the `picture` environment becomes quite powerful.

Although programming pictures directly in LaTeX is severely restricted, and often rather tiresome, there are still reasons for doing so. The documents thus produced are "small" with respect to bytes, and there are no additional graphics files to be dragged along.

This has been the state of things until a few years ago when Till Tantau of beamer fame came up with the Portable Graphics Format pgf and its companion package TikZ (tikz). This system lets you create high quality vector graphics with all current TeX systems including full support for pdf.

Building on these basics, numerous packages have been written for specific purposes. A wide variety of these packages is described in detail in *The LaTeX Graphics Companion* [4].

Perhaps the most advanced graphical tool related with LaTeX is META-POST. It is a stand-alone application based on Donald E. Knuth's META-FONT. METAPOST has the very powerful and mathematically sophisticated programming language of METAFONT but contrary to METAFONT, it generates encapsulated PostScript files, which can be imported in LaTeX and even pdfLaTeX. For an introduction, see *A User's Manual for METAPOST* [15], or the tutorial on [17].

A very thorough discussion of LaTeX and TeX strategies for graphics (and fonts) can be found in *TeX Unbound* [16].

5.2 The picture Environment

By Urs Oswald <osurs@bluewin.ch>

As mentioned above the picture environment is part of standard LaTeX and it is great for simple tasks and also if you want to control the exact positoning of individual elements on a page. But if you are about to do any serious graphics work, you should look at TikZ as presented in section 5.3 on page 115.

5.2.1 Basic Commands

A picture environment[1] is created with one of the two commands

> \begin{picture}(x, y)... \end{picture}

or

> \begin{picture}(x, y) (x_0, y_0)... \end{picture}

The numbers x, y, x_0, y_0 refer to \unitlength, which can be reset any time (but not within a picture environment) with a command such as

> \setlength{\unitlength}{1.2cm}

The default value of \unitlength is 1pt. The first pair, (x, y), effects the reservation, within the document, of rectangular space for the picture. The optional second pair, (x_0, y_0), assigns arbitrary coordinates to the bottom left corner of the reserved rectangle.

---

[1] Believe it or not, the picture environment works out of the box, with standard LaTeX 2_ε no package loading necessary.

Most drawing commands have one of the two forms

$\boxed{\texttt{\textbackslash put}\,(x,y)\,\{\textit{object}\}}$

or

$\boxed{\texttt{\textbackslash multiput}\,(x,y)\,(\Delta x, \Delta y)\,\{n\}\{\textit{object}\}}$

Bézier curves are an exception. They are drawn with the command

$\boxed{\texttt{\textbackslash qbezier}\,(x_1,y_1)\,(x_2,y_2)\,(x_3,y_3)}$

5.2.2   Line Segments

```
\setlength{\unitlength}{5cm}
\begin{picture}(1,1)
  \put(0,0){\line(0,1){1}}
  \put(0,0){\line(1,0){1}}
  \put(0,0){\line(1,1){1}}
  \put(0,0){\line(1,2){.5}}
  \put(0,0){\line(1,3){.3333}}
  \put(0,0){\line(1,4){.25}}
  \put(0,0){\line(1,5){.2}}
  \put(0,0){\line(1,6){.1667}}
  \put(0,0){\line(2,1){1}}
  \put(0,0){\line(2,3){.6667}}
  \put(0,0){\line(2,5){.4}}
  \put(0,0){\line(3,1){1}}
  \put(0,0){\line(3,2){1}}
  \put(0,0){\line(3,4){.75}}
  \put(0,0){\line(3,5){.6}}
  \put(0,0){\line(4,1){1}}
  \put(0,0){\line(4,3){1}}
  \put(0,0){\line(4,5){.8}}
  \put(0,0){\line(5,1){1}}
  \put(0,0){\line(5,2){1}}
  \put(0,0){\line(5,3){1}}
  \put(0,0){\line(5,4){1}}
  \put(0,0){\line(5,6){.8333}}
  \put(0,0){\line(6,1){1}}
  \put(0,0){\line(6,5){1}}
\end{picture}
```

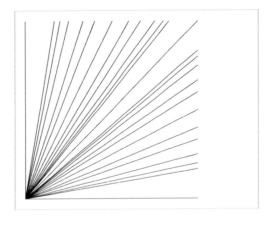

Line segments are drawn with the command

$\put(x,y)\{\line(x_1,y_1)\{\textit{length}\}\}$

The \line command has two arguments:

1. a direction vector,

2. a length.

The components of the direction vector are restricted to the integers

$$-6,\ -5,\ \ldots,\ 5,\ 6,$$

and they have to be coprime (no common divisor except 1). The figure illustrates all 25 possible slope values in the first quadrant. The length is relative to \unitlength. The length argument is the vertical coordinate in the case of a vertical line segment, the horizontal coordinate in all other cases.

5.2.3   Arrows

```
\setlength{\unitlength}{0.75mm}
\begin{picture}(60,40)
  \put(30,20){\vector(1,0){30}}
  \put(30,20){\vector(4,1){20}}
  \put(30,20){\vector(3,1){25}}
  \put(30,20){\vector(2,1){30}}
  \put(30,20){\vector(1,2){10}}
  \thicklines
  \put(30,20){\vector(-4,1){30}}
  \put(30,20){\vector(-1,4){5}}
  \thinlines
  \put(30,20){\vector(-1,-1){5}}
  \put(30,20){\vector(-1,-4){5}}
\end{picture}
```

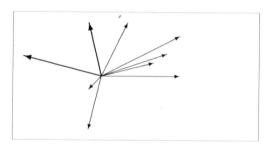

Arrows are drawn with the command

$\put(x,y)\{\vector(x_1,y_1)\{\textit{length}\}\}$

For arrows, the components of the direction vector are even more narrowly restricted than for line segments, namely to the integers

$$-4,\ -3,\ \ldots,\ 3,\ 4.$$

Components also have to be coprime (no common divisor except 1). Notice the effect of the \thicklines command on the two arrows pointing to the upper left.

5.2.4 Circles

```
\setlength{\unitlength}{1mm}
\begin{picture}(60, 40)
  \put(20,30){\circle{1}}
  \put(20,30){\circle{2}}
  \put(20,30){\circle{4}}
  \put(20,30){\circle{8}}
  \put(20,30){\circle{16}}
  \put(20,30){\circle{32}}

  \put(40,30){\circle{1}}
  \put(40,30){\circle{2}}
  \put(40,30){\circle{3}}
  \put(40,30){\circle{4}}
  \put(40,30){\circle{5}}
  \put(40,30){\circle{6}}
  \put(40,30){\circle{7}}
  \put(40,30){\circle{8}}
  \put(40,30){\circle{9}}
  \put(40,30){\circle{10}}
  \put(40,30){\circle{11}}
  \put(40,30){\circle{12}}
  \put(40,30){\circle{13}}
  \put(40,30){\circle{14}}

  \put(15,10){\circle*{1}}
  \put(20,10){\circle*{2}}
  \put(25,10){\circle*{3}}
  \put(30,10){\circle*{4}}
  \put(35,10){\circle*{5}}
\end{picture}
```

The command

```
\put(x,y){\circle{diameter}}
```

draws a circle with center (x,y) and diameter (not radius) *diameter*. The picture environment only admits diameters up to approximately 14 mm, and even below this limit, not all diameters are possible. The `\circle*` command produces disks (filled circles).

As in the case of line segments, one may have to resort to additional packages, such as eepic or pstricks. For a thorough description of these packages, see *The LaTeX Graphics Companion* [4].

There is also a possibility within the picture environment. If one is not afraid of doing the necessary calculations (or leaving them to a program), arbitrary circles and ellipses can be patched together from quadratic Bézier curves. See *Graphics in LaTeX 2ε* [17] for examples and Java source files.

5.2.5   Text and Formulas

```
\setlength{\unitlength}{0.8cm}
\begin{picture}(6,5)
  \thicklines
  \put(1,0.5){\line(2,1){3}}
  \put(4,2){\line(-2,1){2}}
  \put(2,3){\line(-2,-5){1}}
  \put(0.7,0.3){$A$}
  \put(4.05,1.9){$B$}
  \put(1.7,2.95){$C$}
  \put(3.1,2.5){$a$}
  \put(1.3,1.7){$b$}
  \put(2.5,1.05){$c$}
  \put(0.3,4){$F=
    \sqrt{s(s-a)(s-b)(s-c)}$}
  \put(3.5,0.4){$\displaystyle
    s:=\frac{a+b+c}{2}$}
\end{picture}
```

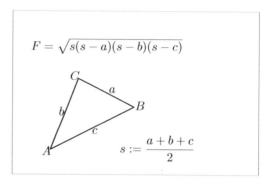

As this example shows, text and formulas can be written into a `picture` environment with the \put command in the usual way.

5.2.6   \multiput and \linethickness

```
\setlength{\unitlength}{2mm}
\begin{picture}(30,20)
  \linethickness{0.075mm}
  \multiput(0,0)(1,0){26}%
    {\line(0,1){20}}
  \multiput(0,0)(0,1){21}%
    {\line(1,0){25}}
  \linethickness{0.15mm}
  \multiput(0,0)(5,0){6}%
    {\line(0,1){20}}
  \multiput(0,0)(0,5){5}%
    {\line(1,0){25}}
  \linethickness{0.3mm}
  \multiput(5,0)(10,0){2}%
    {\line(0,1){20}}
  \multiput(0,5)(0,10){2}%
    {\line(1,0){25}}
\end{picture}
```

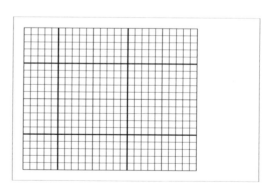

The command

$$\boxed{\texttt{\textbackslash multiput}(x,y)(\Delta x,\Delta y)\{n\}\{object\}}$$

has 4 arguments: the starting point, the translation vector from one object

to the next, the number of objects, and the object to be drawn. The
\linethickness command applies to horizontal and vertical line segments,
but neither to oblique line segments, nor to circles. It does, however, apply
to quadratic Bézier curves!

5.2.7   Ovals

```
\setlength{\unitlength}{0.75cm}
\begin{picture}(6,4)
  \linethickness{0.075mm}
  \multiput(0,0)(1,0){7}%
    {\line(0,1){4}}
  \multiput(0,0)(0,1){5}%
    {\line(1,0){6}}
  \thicklines
  \put(2,3){\oval(3,1.8)}
  \thinlines
  \put(3,2){\oval(3,1.8)}
  \thicklines
  \put(2,1){\oval(3,1.8)[tl]}
  \put(4,1){\oval(3,1.8)[b]}
  \put(4,3){\oval(3,1.8)[r]}
  \put(3,1.5){\oval(1.8,0.4)}
\end{picture}
```

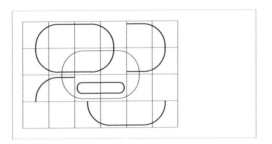

The command

$$\texttt{\textbackslash put}(x,y)\texttt{\{\textbackslash oval}(w,h)\}$$

or

$$\texttt{\textbackslash put}(x,y)\texttt{\{\textbackslash oval}(w,h)\;[\mathit{position}]\}$$

produces an oval centered at (x,y) and having width w and height h. The
optional *position* arguments b, t, l, r refer to "top", "bottom", "left", "right",
and can be combined, as the example illustrates.

Line thickness can be controlled by two kinds of commands:
\linethickness{*length*} on the one hand, \thinlines and \thicklines
on the other. While \linethickness{*length*} applies only to horizontal and
vertical lines (and quadratic Bézier curves), \thinlines and \thicklines
apply to oblique line segments as well as to circles and ovals.

5.2.8   Multiple Use of Predefined Picture Boxes

```
\setlength{\unitlength}{0.5mm}
\begin{picture}(120,168)
\newsavebox{\foldera}
\savebox{\foldera}
  (40,32)[bl]{% definition
  \multiput(0,0)(0,28){2}
    {\line(1,0){40}}
  \multiput(0,0)(40,0){2}
    {\line(0,1){28}}
  \put(1,28){\oval(2,2)[tl]}
  \put(1,29){\line(1,0){5}}
  \put(9,29){\oval(6,6)[tl]}
  \put(9,32){\line(1,0){8}}
  \put(17,29){\oval(6,6)[tr]}
  \put(20,29){\line(1,0){19}}
  \put(39,28){\oval(2,2)[tr]}
}
\newsavebox{\folderb}
\savebox{\folderb}
  (40,32)[l]{%           definition
  \put(0,14){\line(1,0){8}}
  \put(8,0){\usebox{\foldera}}
}
\put(34,26){\line(0,1){102}}
\put(14,128){\usebox{\foldera}}
\multiput(34,86)(0,-37){3}
  {\usebox{\folderb}}
\end{picture}
```

A picture box can be *declared* by the command

> `\newsavebox{`*name*`}`

then *defined* by

> `\savebox{`*name*`}(`*width,height*`)[`*position*`]{`*content*`}`

and finally arbitrarily often be *drawn* by

> `\put(`x, y`){\usebox{`*name*`}}`

The optional *position* parameter has the effect of defining the 'anchor point' of the savebox. In the example it is set to `bl` which puts the anchor point into the bottom left corner of the savebox. The other position specifiers are top and right.

The *name* argument refers to a LATEX storage bin and therefore is of a command nature (which accounts for the backslashes in the current example). Boxed pictures can be nested: In this example, \foldera is used within the definition of \folderb.

The \oval command had to be used as the \line command does not work if the segment length is less than about 3 mm.

5.2.9 Quadratic Bézier Curves

```
\setlength{\unitlength}{0.8cm}
\begin{picture}(6,4)
  \linethickness{0.075mm}
  \multiput(0,0)(1,0){7}
    {\line(0,1){4}}
  \multiput(0,0)(0,1){5}
    {\line(1,0){6}}
  \thicklines
  \put(0.5,0.5){\line(1,5){0.5}}
  \put(1,3){\line(4,1){2}}
  \qbezier(0.5,0.5)(1,3)(3,3.5)
  \thinlines
  \put(2.5,2){\line(2,-1){3}}
  \put(5.5,0.5){\line(-1,5){0.5}}
  \linethickness{1mm}
  \qbezier(2.5,2)(5.5,0.5)(5,3)
  \thinlines
  \qbezier(4,2)(4,3)(3,3)
  \qbezier(3,3)(2,3)(2,2)
  \qbezier(2,2)(2,1)(3,1)
  \qbezier(3,1)(4,1)(4,2)
\end{picture}
```

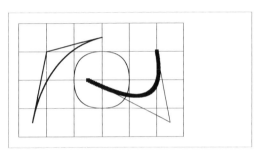

As this example illustrates, splitting up a circle into 4 quadratic Bézier curves is not satisfactory. At least 8 are needed. The figure again shows the effect of the \linethickness command on horizontal or vertical lines, and of the \thinlines and the \thicklines commands on oblique line segments. It also shows that both kinds of commands affect quadratic Bézier curves, each command overriding all previous ones.

Let $P_1 = (x_1, y_1)$, $P_2 = (x_2, y_2)$ denote the end points, and m_1, m_2 the respective slopes, of a quadratic Bézier curve. The intermediate control point $S = (x, y)$ is then given by the equations

$$\begin{cases} rclx = & \dfrac{m_2 x_2 - m_1 x_1 - (y_2 - y_1)}{m_2 - m_1}, \\ y = & y_i + m_i(x - x_i) \qquad (i = 1, 2). \end{cases} \tag{5.1}$$

See *Graphics in LATEX 2ε* [17] for a Java program which generates the necessary \qbezier command line.

5.2.10   Catenary

```
\setlength{\unitlength}{1cm}
\begin{picture}(4.3,3.6)(-2.5,-0.25)
\put(-2,0){\vector(1,0){4.4}}
\put(2.45,-.05){$x$}
\put(0,0){\vector(0,1){3.2}}
\put(0,3.35){\makebox(0,0){$y$}}
\qbezier(0.0,0.0)(1.2384,0.0)
  (2.0,2.7622)
\qbezier(0.0,0.0)(-1.2384,0.0)
  (-2.0,2.7622)
\linethickness{.075mm}
\multiput(-2,0)(1,0){5}
  {\line(0,1){3}}
\multiput(-2,0)(0,1){4}
  {\line(1,0){4}}
\linethickness{.2mm}
\put( .3,.12763){\line(1,0){.4}}
\put(.5,-.07237){\line(0,1){.4}}
\put(-.7,.12763){\line(1,0){.4}}
\put(-.5,-.07237){\line(0,1){.4}}
\put(.8,.54308){\line(1,0){.4}}
\put(1,.34308){\line(0,1){.4}}
\put(-1.2,.54308){\line(1,0){.4}}
\put(-1,.34308){\line(0,1){.4}}
\put(1.3,1.35241){\line(1,0){.4}}
\put(1.5,1.15241){\line(0,1){.4}}
\put(-1.7,1.35241){\line(1,0){.4}}
\put(-1.5,1.15241){\line(0,1){.4}}
\put(-2.5,-0.25){\circle*{0.2}}
\end{picture}
```

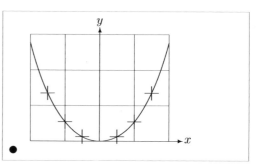

In this figure, each symmetric half of the catenary $y = \cosh x - 1$ is approximated by a quadratic Bézier curve. The right half of the curve ends in the point $(2, 2.7622)$, the slope there having the value $m = 3.6269$. Using again equation (5.1), we can calculate the intermediate control points. They turn out to be $(1.2384, 0)$ and $(-1.2384, 0)$. The crosses indicate points of the *real* catenary. The error is barely noticeable, being less than one percent.

This example points out the use of the optional argument of the \begin{picture} command. The picture is defined in convenient "mathematical" coordinates, whereas by the command

```
\begin{picture}(4.3,3.6)(-2.5,-0.25)
```

its lower left corner (marked by the black disk) is assigned the coordinates $(-2.5, -0.25)$.

5.2.11   Rapidity in the Special Theory of Relativity

```
\setlength{\unitlength}{0.8cm}
\begin{picture}(6,4)(-3,-2)
  \put(-2.5,0){\vector(1,0){5}}
  \put(2.7,-0.1){$\chi$}
  \put(0,-1.5){\vector(0,1){3}}
  \multiput(-2.5,1)(0.4,0){13}
    {\line(1,0){0.2}}
  \multiput(-2.5,-1)(0.4,0){13}
    {\line(1,0){0.2}}
  \put(0.2,1.4)
    {$\beta=v/c=\tanh\chi$}
  \qbezier(0,0)(0.8853,0.8853)
    (2,0.9640)
  \qbezier(0,0)(-0.8853,-0.8853)
    (-2,-0.9640)
  \put(-3,-2){\circle*{0.2}}
\end{picture}
```

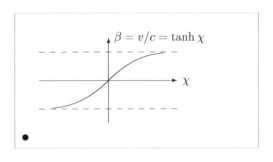

The control points of the two Bézier curves were calculated with formulas (5.1). The positive branch is determined by $P_1 = (0, 0)$, $m_1 = 1$ and $P_2 = (2, \tanh 2)$, $m_2 = 1/\cosh^2 2$. Again, the picture is defined in mathematically convenient coordinates, and the lower left corner is assigned the mathematical coordinates $(-3, -2)$ (black disk).

5.3   The PGF and TikZ Graphics Packages

Today every LaTeX output generation system can create nice vector graphics, it's just the interfaces that are rather diverse. The **pgf** package provides an abstraction layer over these interface. The **pgf** package comes with a large manual/tutorial of its own [18]. So we are only going to scratch the surface of the package with this little section.

The **pgf** package comes with a high level access language provided by the tikz package. TikZ provides highly efficient commands to draw graphics right from inside your document. Use the `tikzpicture` environment to wrap your TikZ commands.

As mentioned above, there is an excellent manual for **pgf** and friends. So instead of actually explaining how it works, I will just show you a few examples so that you can get a first impression of how this tool works.

First a simple nonsense diagram.

```
\begin{tikzpicture}[scale=3]
  \clip (-0.1,-0.2)
      rectangle (1.8,1.2);
  \draw[step=.25cm,gray,very thin]
      (-1.4,-1.4) grid (3.4,3.4);
  \draw (-1.5,0) -- (2.5,0);
  \draw (0,-1.5) -- (0,1.5);
  \draw (0,0) circle (1cm);
  \filldraw[fill=green!20!white,
        draw=green!50!black]
    (0,0) -- (3mm,0mm)
        arc (0:30:3mm) -- cycle;
\end{tikzpicture}
```

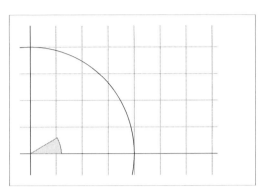

Note the semicolon (;) character. It separates the individual commands.

A simple Venn diagram.

```
\shorthandoff{:}
\begin{tikzpicture}
  \node[circle,draw,
        minimum size=3cm,
        label=120:{economics}]
      at (0,0) {};
  \node[circle,draw,
        minimum size=3cm,
        label=60:{psychology}]
      at (1,0) {};
  \node (i) at (0.5,-1) {};
  \node at (0.6,-2.5)
    {behavioral economics}
    edge[->,thick,
        out=60,in=-60] (i);
\end{tikzpicture}
```

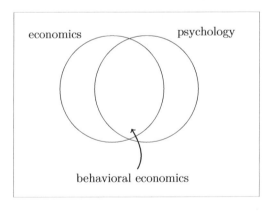

If you are using tikz in connection with babel some of the characters used in the TikZ language may get modified by babel, leading to odd errors. To counteract this, add the \shorthandoff command to your code.

Note the foreach loops in the next example.

```
\begin{tikzpicture}[scale=0.8]
  \tikzstyle{v}=[circle, minimum size=2mm,inner sep=0pt,draw]
  \foreach \i in {1,...,8}
    \foreach \j in {1,...,3}
      \node[v]
        (G-\i-\j) at (\i,\j) {};
  \foreach \i in {1,...,8}
    \foreach \j/\o in {1/2,2/3}
      \draw[->]
        (G-\i-\j) -- (G-\i-\o);
  \foreach \i/\n in
    {1/2,2/3,3/4,4/5,5/6,6/7,7/8}
    \foreach \j/\o in {1/2,2/3} {
        \draw[->] (G-\i-\j) -- (G-\n-\o);
        \draw[->] (G-\n-\j) -- (G-\i-\o);
    }
\end{tikzpicture}
```

With the \usetikzlibrary command in the preamble you can enable a wide variety of additional features for drawing special shapes, like this box which is slightly bent.

```
\usetikzlibrary{%
  decorations.pathmorphing}
\begin{tikzpicture}[
    decoration={bent,aspect=.3}]
\draw [decorate,fill=lightgray]
      (0,0) rectangle (5.5,4);
\node[circle,draw]
      (A) at (.5,.5) {A};
\node[circle,draw]
      (B) at (5,3.5) {B};
\draw[->,decorate] (A) -- (B);
\draw[->,decorate] (B) -- (A);
\end{tikzpicture}
```

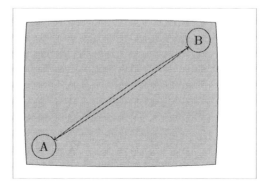

```
\usetikzlibrary{positioning}
\begin{tikzpicture}[xscale=6,
    yscale=8,>=stealth]
  \tikzstyle{v}=[circle,
    minimum size=1mm,draw,thick]
  \node[v] (a) {$1$};
  \node[v] (b) [right=of a] {$2$};
  \node[v] (c) [below=of a] {$2$};
  \node[v] (d) [below=of b] {$1$};
  \draw[thick,->]
        (a) to node {} (c);
  \draw[thick,->]
        (a) to node {} (d);
  \draw[thick,->]
        (b) to node {} (d);
\end{tikzpicture}
```

You can even draw syntax diagrams that look as if they came straight from a book on Pascal programming. The code is a bit more daunting than the example above, so I will just show you the result. If you have a look at the pgf documentation you will find a detailed tutorial on drawing this exact diagram.

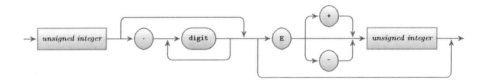

And there is more, if you have to draw plots of numerical data or functions, you should have a closer look at the **pgfplot** package. It provides everything you need to draw plots. It can even call the external **gnuplot** command to evaluate actual functions you wrote into the graph.

For more inspiration make sure to visit Kjell Magne Fauske's excellent http://www.texample.net/tikz/. it contains an ever expanding store of beautiful graphs and other LATEX code. On TEXample.net you will also find a list of tools to work with PGF/TikZ so that you do not have to write all that code by hand.

Chapter 6

Customising LaTeX

Documents produced with the commands you have learned up to this point will look acceptable to a large audience. While they are not fancy-looking, they obey all the established rules of good typesetting, which will make them easy to read and pleasant to look at.

However, there are situations where LaTeX does not provide a command or environment that matches your needs, or the output produced by some existing command may not meet your requirements.

In this chapter, I will try to give some hints on how to teach LaTeX new tricks and how to make it produce output that looks different from what is provided by default.

6.1   New Commands, Environments and Packages

You may have noticed that all the commands I introduce in this book are typeset in a box, and that they show up in the index at the end of the book. Instead of directly using the necessary LaTeX commands to achieve this, I have created a package in which I defined new commands and environments for this purpose. Now I can simply write:

```
\begin{lscommand}
\ci{dum}
\end{lscommand}
```

> \dum

In this example, I am using both a new environment called `lscommand`, which is responsible for drawing the box around the command, and a new command named `\ci`, which typesets the command name and makes a corresponding entry in the index. Check this out by looking up the `\dum` command in the index at the back of this book, where you'll find an entry for `\dum`, pointing to every page where I mentioned the `\dum` command.

If I ever decide that I do not like having the commands typeset in a box any more, I can simply change the definition of the `lscommand` environment to create a new look. This is much easier than going through the whole document to hunt down all the places where I have used some generic LaTeX commands to draw a box around some word.

6.1.1 New Commands

To add your own commands, use the

> \newcommand{*name*}[*num*]{*definition*}

command. Basically, the command requires two arguments: the *name* of the command you want to create, and the *definition* of the command. The *num* argument in square brackets is optional and specifies the number of arguments the new command takes (up to 9 are possible). If missing it defaults to 0, i.e. no argument allowed.

The following two examples should help you to get the idea. The first example defines a new command called \tnss. This is short for "The Not So Short Introduction to LaTeX 2_ε." Such a command could come in handy if you had to write the title of this book over and over again.

```
\newcommand{\tnss}{The not
    so Short Introduction to
    \LaTeXe}
This is ''\tnss'' \ldots{}
''\tnss''
```

> This is "The not so Short Introduction to LaTeX 2_ε" ... "The not so Short Introduction to LaTeX 2_ε"

The next example illustrates how to define a new command that takes one argument. The #1 tag gets replaced by the argument you specify. If you wanted to use more than one argument, use #2 and so on.

```
\newcommand{\txsit}[2]
 {This is the \emph{#1}
  #2 Introduction to \LaTeXe}
% in the document body:
\begin{itemize}
\item \txsit{not so}{short}
\item \txsit{very}{long}
\end{itemize}
```

> - This is the *not so* short Introduction to LaTeX 2_ε
> - This is the *very* long Introduction to LaTeX 2_ε

LaTeX will not allow you to create a new command that would overwrite an existing one. But there is a special command in case you explicitly want this: \renewcommand. It uses the same syntax as the \newcommand command.

In certain cases you might also want to use the \providecommand command. It works like \newcommand, but if the command is already defined, LATEX 2_ε will silently ignore it.

There are some points to note about whitespace following LATEX commands. See page 5 for more information.

6.1.2 New Environments

Just as with the \newcommand command, there is a command to create your own environments. The \newenvironment command uses the following syntax:

```
\newenvironment{name}[num]{before}{after}
```

Again \newenvironment can have an optional argument. The material specified in the *before* argument is processed before the text in the environment gets processed. The material in the *after* argument gets processed when the \end{*name*} command is encountered.

The example below illustrates the usage of the \newenvironment command.

```
\newenvironment{king}
 {\rule{1ex}{1ex}%
     \hspace{\stretch{1}}}
 {\hspace{\stretch{1}}%
     \rule{1ex}{1ex}}

\begin{king}
My humble subjects \ldots
\end{king}
```

■   My humble subjects ...   ■

The *num* argument is used the same way as in the \newcommand command. LATEX makes sure that you do not define an environment that already exists. If you ever want to change an existing command, use the \renewenvironment command. It uses the same syntax as the \newenvironment command.

The commands used in this example will be explained later. For the \rule command see page 135, for \stretch go to page 129, and more information on \hspace can be found on page 129.

6.1.3 Extra Space

When creating a new environment you may easily get bitten by extra spaces creeping in, which can potentially have fatal effects, for example when you want to create a title environment which supresses its own indentation as well as the one on the following paragraph. The \ignorespaces command in the begin block of the environment will make it ignore any space after executing the begin block. The end block is a bit more tricky as special processing occurs at the end of an environment. With the `\ignorespacesafterend` LaTeX will issue an `\ignorespaces` after the special 'end' processing has occured.

```
\newenvironment{simple}%
 {\noindent}%
 {\par\noindent}

\begin{simple}
See the space\\to the left.
\end{simple}
Same\\here.
```

> See the space
> to the left.
>
> Same
> here.

```
\newenvironment{correct}%
 {\noindent\ignorespaces}%
 {\par\noindent%
   \ignorespacesafterend}

\begin{correct}
No space\\to the left.
\end{correct}
Same\\here.
```

> No space
> to the left.
>
> Same
> here.

6.1.4   Commandline LaTeX

If you work on a Unix-like OS, you might be using Makefiles to build your LaTeX projects. In that connection it might be interesting to produce different versions of the same document by calling LaTeX with commandline parameters. If you add the following structure to your document:

```
\usepackage{ifthen}
\ifthenelse{\equal{\blackandwhite}{true}}{
  % "black and white" mode; do something..
}{
  % "color" mode; do something different..
}
```

Now call LaTeX like this:

```
latex '\newcommand{\blackandwhite}{true}\input{test.tex}'
```

First the command `\blackandwhite` gets defined and then the actual file is read with input. By setting `\blackandwhite` to false the color version of the document would be produced.

6.1.5 Your Own Package

If you define a lot of new environments and commands, the preamble of your document will get quite long. In this situation, it is a good idea to create a LaTeX package containing all your command and environment definitions. Use the \usepackage command to make the package available in your document.

```
% Demo Package by Tobias Oetiker
\ProvidesPackage{demopack}
\newcommand{\tnss}{The not so Short Introduction
                   to \LaTeXe}
\newcommand{\txsit}[1]{The \emph{#1} Short
                      Introduction to \LaTeXe}
\newenvironment{king}{\begin{quote}}{\end{quote}}
```

Figure 6.1: Example Package.

Writing a package basically consists of copying the contents of your document preamble into a separate file with a name ending in .sty. There is one special command,

```
\ProvidesPackage{package name}
```

for use at the very beginning of your package file. \ProvidesPackage tells LaTeX the name of the package and will allow it to issue a sensible error message when you try to include a package twice. Figure 6.1 shows a small example package that contains the commands defined in the examples above.

6.2   Fonts and Sizes

6.2.1   Font Changing Commands

LaTeX chooses the appropriate font and font size based on the logical structure of the document (sections, footnotes, ...). In some cases, one might like to change fonts and sizes by hand. To do this, use the commands listed in Tables 6.1 and 6.2. The actual size of each font is a design issue and depends on the document class and its options. Table 6.3 shows the absolute point size for these commands as implemented in the standard document classes.

```
{\small The small and
\textbf{bold} Romans ruled}
{\Large all of great big
\textit{Italy}.}
```

The small and **bold** Romans ruled all of great big *Italy.*

One important feature of LaTeX 2_ε is that the font attributes are independent. This means that issuing size or even font changing commands, and still keep bold or slant attributes set earlier.

In *math mode* use the font changing *commands* to temporarily exit *math mode* and enter some normal text. If you want to switch to another font for math typesetting you need another special set of commands; refer to Table 6.4.

In connection with the font size commands, curly braces play a significant role. They are used to build *groups*. Groups limit the scope of most LaTeX commands.

```
He likes {\LARGE large and
{\small small} letters}.
```

He likes large and small letters.

The font size commands also change the line spacing, but only if the paragraph ends within the scope of the font size command. The closing curly brace } should therefore not come too early. Note the position of the \par command in the next two examples. [1]

---

[1] \par is equivalent to a blank line

Table 6.1: Fonts.

\textrm{...}	roman	\textsf{...}	sans serif
\texttt{...}	typewriter		
\textmd{...}	medium	\textbf{...}	**bold face**
\textup{...}	upright	\textit{...}	*italic*
\textsl{...}	*slanted*	\textsc{...}	SMALL CAPS
\emph{...}	*emphasized*	\textnormal{...}	document font

Table 6.2: Font Sizes.

\tiny	tiny font	\Large	larger font
\scriptsize	very small font	\LARGE	very large font
\footnotesize	quite small font		
\small	small font	\huge	huge
\normalsize	normal font		
\large	large font	\Huge	largest

Table 6.3: Absolute Point Sizes in Standard Classes.

size	10pt (default)	11pt option	12pt option
\tiny	5pt	6pt	6pt
\scriptsize	7pt	8pt	8pt
\footnotesize	8pt	9pt	10pt
\small	9pt	10pt	11pt
\normalsize	10pt	11pt	12pt
\large	12pt	12pt	14pt
\Large	14pt	14pt	17pt
\LARGE	17pt	17pt	20pt
\huge	20pt	20pt	25pt
\Huge	25pt	25pt	25pt

Table 6.4: Math Fonts.

\mathrm{...}	Roman Font
\mathbf{...}	**Boldface Font**
\mathsf{...}	Sans Serif Font
\mathtt{...}	Typewriter Font
\mathit{...}	*Italic Font*
\mathcal{...}	$\mathcal{CALLIGRAPHIC\ FONT}$
\mathnormal{...}	*Normal Font*

```
{\Large Don't read this!
 It is not true.
 You can believe me!\par}
```

Don't read this! It is not true.
You can believe me!

```
{\Large This is not true either.
But remember I am a liar.}\par
```

This is not true either. But
remember I am a liar.

If you want to activate a size changing command for a whole paragraph
of text or even more, you might want to use the environment syntax for font
changing commands.

```
\begin{Large}
This is not true.
But then again, what is these
days \ldots
\end{Large}
```

This is not true. But then
again, what is these days ...

This will save you from counting lots of curly braces.

6.2.2   Danger, Will Robinson, Danger

As noted at the beginning of this chapter, it is dangerous to clutter your
document with explicit commands like this, because they work in opposition
to the basic idea of LATEX, which is to separate the logical and visual markup
of your document. This means that if you use the same font changing
command in several places in order to typeset a special kind of information,
you should use \newcommand to define a "logical wrapper command" for the
font changing command.

```
\newcommand{\oops}[1]{%
 \textbf{#1}}
Do not \oops{enter} this room,
it's occupied by \oops{machines}
of unknown origin and purpose.
```

Do not **enter** this room, it's occupied by
machines of unknown origin and purpose.

This approach has the advantage that you can decide at some later
stage that you want to use a visual representation of danger other than
\textbf, without having to wade through your document, identifying all the
occurrences of \textbf and then figuring out for each one whether it was
used for pointing out danger or for some other reason.

Please note the difference between telling LATEX to *emphasize* something
and telling it to use a different *font*. The \emph command is context aware,
while the font commands are absolute.

```
\textit{You can also
  \emph{emphasize} text if
  it is set in italics,}
\textsf{in a
  \emph{sans-serif} font,}
\texttt{or in
  \emph{typewriter} style.}
```

You can also emphasize *text if it is set in italics*, in a *sans-serif* font, or in *typewriter* style.

6.2.3 Advice

To conclude this journey into the land of fonts and font sizes, here is a little word of advice:

Remember! *The* M**O** R*E* fonts y**o**u ᵤₛₑ **in** a document, *the* more READABLE and *beautiful it* becomeS.

6.3 Spacing

6.3.1 Line Spacing

If you want to use larger inter-line spacing in a document, change its value by putting the

```
\linespread{factor}
```

command into the preamble of your document. Use `\linespread{1.3}` for "one and a half" line spacing, and `\linespread{1.6}` for "double" line spacing. Normally the lines are not spread, so the default line spread factor is 1.

Note that the effect of the `\linespread` command is rather drastic and not appropriate for published work. So if you have a good reason for changing the line spacing you might want to use the command:

```
\setlength{\baselineskip}{1.5\baselineskip}
```

```
{\setlength{\baselineskip}%
        {1.5\baselineskip}
This paragraph is typeset with
the baseline skip set to 1.5 of
what it was before. Note the par
command at the end of the
paragraph.\par}

This paragraph has a clear
purpose, it shows that after the
curly brace has been closed,
everything is back to normal.
```

This paragraph is typeset with the baseline skip set to 1.5 of what it was before. Note the par command at the end of the paragraph.

This paragraph has a clear purpose, it shows that after the curly brace has been closed, everything is back to normal.

6.3.2 Paragraph Formatting

In LaTeX, there are two parameters influencing paragraph layout. By placing a definition like

```
\setlength{\parindent}{0pt}
\setlength{\parskip}{1ex plus 0.5ex minus 0.2ex}
```

in the preamble of the input file, you can change the layout of paragraphs. These two commands increase the space between two paragraphs while setting the paragraph indent to zero.

The plus and minus parts of the length above tell TeX that it can compress and expand the inter-paragraph skip by the amount specified, if this is necessary to properly fit the paragraphs onto the page.

In continental Europe, paragraphs are often separated by some space and not indented. But beware, this also has its effect on the table of contents. Its lines get spaced more loosely now as well. To avoid this, you might want to move the two commands from the preamble into your document to some place below the command \tableofcontents or to not use them at all, because you'll find that most professional books use indenting and not spacing to separate paragraphs.

If you want to indent a paragraph that is not indented, use

```
\indent
```

at the beginning of the paragraph.[2] Obviously, this will only have an effect when \parindent is not set to zero.

To create a non-indented paragraph, use

```
\noindent
```

as the first command of the paragraph. This might come in handy when you start a document with body text and not with a sectioning command.

6.3.3 Horizontal Space

LaTeX determines the spaces between words and sentences automatically. To add horizontal space, use:

```
\hspace{length}
```

If such a space should be kept even if it falls at the end or the start of a line, use \hspace* instead of \hspace. The *length* in the simplest case is just a number plus a unit. The most important units are listed in Table 6.5.

```
This\hspace{1.5cm}is a space
of 1.5 cm.
```

> This   is a space of 1.5 cm.

The command

```
\stretch{n}
```

generates a special rubber space. It stretches until all the remaining space on a line is filled up. If multiple \hspace{\stretch{n}} commands are issued on the same line, they occupy all available space in proportion of their respective stretch factors.

```
x\hspace{\stretch{1}}
x\hspace{\stretch{3}}x
```

When using horizontal space together with text, it may make sense to make the space adjust its size relative to the size of the current font. This can be done by using the text-relative units em and ex:

---

[2]To indent the first paragraph after each section head, use the indentfirst package in the 'tools' bundle.

Table 6.5: TeX Units.

mm	millimetre $\approx 1/25$ inch	⌴
cm	centimetre $= 10$ mm	∟____⌐
in	inch $= 25.4$ mm	∟_____⌐
pt	point $\approx 1/72$ inch $\approx \frac{1}{3}$ mm	‖
em	approx width of an 'M' in the current font	⌴__⌐
ex	approx height of an 'x' in the current font	⌴

```
{\Large{}big\hspace{1em}y}\\
{\tiny{}tin\hspace{1em}y}
```

big   y

tin y

6.3.4 Vertical Space

The space between paragraphs, sections, subsections, ... is determined automatically by LaTeX. If necessary, additional vertical space *between two paragraphs* can be added with the command:

    \vspace{*length*}

This command should normally be used between two empty lines. If the space should be preserved at the top or at the bottom of a page, use the starred version of the command, \vspace*, instead of \vspace.

The \stretch command, in connection with \pagebreak, can be used to typeset text on the last line of a page, or to centre text vertically on a page.

```
Some text \ldots

\vspace{\stretch{1}}
This goes onto the last line of the page.\pagebreak
```

Additional space between two lines of *the same* paragraph or within a table is specified with the

    \\[*length*]

command.

With \bigskip and \smallskip you can skip a predefined amount of vertical space without having to worry about exact numbers.

6.4   Page Layout

LaTeX 2_ε allows you to specify the paper size in the \documentclass command. It then automatically picks the right text margins, but sometimes you may not be happy with the predefined values. Naturally, you can change them. Figure 6.2 shows all the parameters that can be changed. The figure was produced with the layout package from the tools bundle.[3]

WAIT! . . . before you launch into a "Let's make that narrow page a bit wider" frenzy, take a few seconds to think. As with most things in LaTeX, there is a good reason for the page layout to be as it is.

Sure, compared to your off-the-shelf MS Word page, it looks awfully narrow. But take a look at your favourite book[4] and count the number of characters on a standard text line. You will find that there are no more than about 66 characters on each line. Now do the same on your LaTeX page. You will find that there are also about 66 characters per line. Experience shows that the reading gets difficult as soon as there are more characters on a single line. This is because it is difficult for the eyes to move from the end of one line to the start of the next one. This is also why newspapers are typeset in multiple columns.

So if you increase the width of your body text, keep in mind that you are making life difficult for the readers of your paper. But enough of the cautioning, I promised to tell you how you do it . . .

LaTeX provides two commands to change these parameters. They are usually used in the document preamble.

The first command assigns a fixed value to any of the parameters:

> \setlength{*parameter*}{*length*}

The second command adds a length to any of the parameters:

> \addtolength{*parameter*}{*length*}

This second command is actually more useful than the \setlength command, because it works relative to the existing settings. To add one centimetre to the overall text width, I put the following commands into the document preamble:

```
\addtolength{\hoffset}{-0.5cm}
\addtolength{\textwidth}{1cm}
```

In this context, you might want to look at the calc package. It allows you to use arithmetic operations in the argument of \setlength and other places where numeric values are entered into function arguments.

---

[3]`pkg/tools`
[4]I mean a real printed book produced by a reputable publisher.

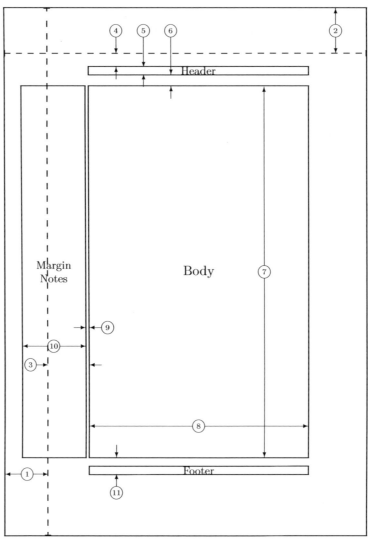

Figure 6.2: Layout parameters for this book. Try the layouts package to print the layout of your own document.

6.5   More Fun With Lengths

Whenever possible, I avoid using absolute lengths in LaTeX documents. I rather try to base things on the width or height of other page elements. For the width of a figure this could be `\textwidth` in order to make it fill the page.

The following 3 commands allow you to determine the width, height and depth of a text string.

```
\settoheight{variable}{text}
\settodepth{variable}{text}
\settowidth{variable}{text}
```

The example below shows a possible application of these commands.

```
\flushleft
\newenvironment{vardesc}[1]{%
  \settowidth{\parindent}{#1:\ }
  \makebox[0pt][r]{#1:\ }}{}

\begin{displaymath}
a^2+b^2=c^2
\end{displaymath}

\begin{vardesc}{Where}$a$,
$b$ -- are adjacent to the right
angle of a right-angled triangle.

$c$ -- is the hypotenuse of
the triangle and feels lonely.

$d$ -- finally does not show up
here at all. Isn't that puzzling?
\end{vardesc}
```

$$a^2 + b^2 = c^2$$

Where: a, b – are adjacent to the right angle of a right-angled triangle.

c – is the hypotenuse of the triangle and feels lonely.

d – finally does not show up here at all. Isn't that puzzling?

6.6   Boxes

LaTeX builds up its pages by pushing around boxes. At first, each letter is a little box, which is then glued to other letters to form words. These are again glued to other words, but with special glue, which is elastic so that a series of words can be squeezed or stretched as to exactly fill a line on the page.

I admit, this is a very simplistic version of what really happens, but the point is that TeX operates on glue and boxes. Letters are not the only things that can be boxes. You can put virtually everything into a box, including other boxes. Each box will then be handled by LATEX as if it were a single letter.

In earlier chapters you encountered some boxes, although I did not tell you. The `tabular` environment and the `\includegraphics`, for example, both produce a box. This means that you can easily arrange two tables or images side by side. You just have to make sure that their combined width is not larger than the textwidth.

You can also pack a paragraph of your choice into a box with either the

`\parbox[`*pos*`]{`*width*`}{`*text*`}`

command or the

`\begin{minipage}[`*pos*`]{`*width*`}` text `\end{minipage}`

environment. The `pos` parameter can take one of the letters `c`, `t` or `b` to control the vertical alignment of the box, relative to the baseline of the surrounding text. `width` takes a length argument specifying the width of the box. The main difference between a `minipage` and a `\parbox` is that you cannot use all commands and environments inside a `parbox`, while almost anything is possible in a `minipage`.

While `\parbox` packs up a whole paragraph doing line breaking and everything, there is also a class of boxing commands that operates only on horizontally aligned material. We already know one of them; it's called `\mbox`. It simply packs up a series of boxes into another one, and can be used to prevent LATEX from breaking two words. As boxes can be put inside boxes, these horizontal box packers give you ultimate flexibility.

`\makebox[`*width*`]` `[`*pos*`]{`*text*`}`

`width` defines the width of the resulting box as seen from the outside.[5] Besides the length expressions, you can also use `\width`, `\height`, `\depth`, and `\totalheight` in the width parameter. They are set from values obtained by measuring the typeset *text*. The *pos* parameter takes a one letter value: center, flushleft, flushright, or spread the text to fill the box.

The command `\framebox` works exactly the same as `\makebox`, but it draws a box around the text.

The following example shows you some things you could do with the `\makebox` and `\framebox` commands.

---

[5]This means it can be smaller than the material inside the box. You can even set the width to 0pt so that the text inside the box will be typeset without influencing the surrounding boxes.

```
\makebox[\textwidth]{%
    c e n t r a l}\par
\makebox[\textwidth][s]{%
    s p r e a d}\par
\framebox[1.1\width]{Guess I'm
    framed now!} \par
\framebox[0.8\width][r]{Bummer,
    I am too wide} \par
\framebox[1cm][l]{never
    mind, so am I}
Can you read this?
```

Now that we control the horizontal, the obvious next step is to go for the vertical.[6] No problem for LaTeX. The

```
\raisebox{lift}[extend-above-baseline][extend-below-baseline]{text}
```

command lets you define the vertical properties of a box. You can use \width, \height, \depth, and \totalheight in the first three parameters, in order to act upon the size of the box inside the *text* argument.

```
\raisebox{0pt}[0pt][0pt]{\Large%
\textbf{Aaaa\raisebox{-0.3ex}{a}%
\raisebox{-0.7ex}{aa}%
\raisebox{-1.2ex}{r}%
\raisebox{-2.2ex}{g}%
\raisebox{-4.5ex}{h}}}
she shouted, but not even the next
one in line noticed that something
terrible had happened to her.
```

6.7 Rules

A few pages back you may have noticed the command

```
\rule[lift]{width}{height}
```

In normal use it produces a simple black box.

```
\rule{3mm}{.1pt}%
\rule[-1mm]{5mm}{1cm}%
\rule{3mm}{.1pt}%
\rule[1mm]{1cm}{5mm}%
\rule{3mm}{.1pt}
```

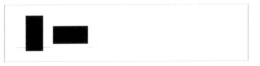

---

[6]Total control is only to be obtained by controlling both the horizontal and the vertical
...

This is useful for drawing vertical and horizontal lines. The line on the title page, for example, has been created with a `\rule` command.

The End.

Appendix A

Installing LaTeX

Knuth published the source to TeX back in a time when nobody knew about OpenSource and/or Free Software. The License that comes with TeX lets you do whatever you want with the source, but you can only call the result of your work TeX if the program passes a set of tests Knuth has also provided. This has lead to a situation where we have free TeX implementations for almost every Operating System under the sun. This chapter will give some hints on what to install on Linux, Mac OS X and Windows, to get a working TeX setup.

A.1 What to Install

To use LaTeX on any computer system, you need several programs.

1. The TeX/LaTeX program for processing your LaTeX source files into typeset PDF or DVI documents.

2. A text editor for editing your LaTeX source files. Some products even let you start the LaTeX program from within the editor.

3. A PDF/DVI viewer program for previewing and printing your documents.

4. A program to handle POSTSCRIPT files and images for inclusion into your documents.

For every platforms there are several programs that fit the requirements above. Here we just tell about the ones we know, like and have some experience with.

A.2 Cross Platform Editor

While TeX is available on many different computing platforms, LaTeX editors have long been highly platform specific.

Over the past few years I have come to like Texmaker quite a lot. Apart from being very a useful editor with integrated pdf-preview and syntax highlighting, it has the advantage of running on Windows, Mac and Unix/Linux equally well. See `http://www.xm1math.net/texmaker` for further information. There is also a forked version of Texmaker called TeXstudio on `http://texstudio.sourceforge.net/`. It also seems well maintained and is also available for all three major platforms.

You will find some platform specific editor suggestions in the OS sections below.

A.3　TeX on Mac OS X

A.3.1　TeX Distribution

Just download MacTeX. It is a pre-compiled LaTeX distribution for OS X. MacTeX provides a full LaTeX installation plus a number of additional tools. Get MacTeX from `http://www.tug.org/mactex/`.

A.3.2　OSX TeX Editor

If you are not happy with our crossplatform suggestion Texmaker (section A.2).

The most popular open source editor for LaTeX on the mac seems to be TeXshop. Get a copy from `http://www.uoregon.edu/~koch/texshop`. It is also contained in the MacTeX distribution.

Recent TeXLive distributions contain the TeXworks editor `http://texworks.org/` which is a multi-platform editor based on the TeXShop design. Since TeXworks uses the Qt toolkit, it is available on any platform supported by this toolkit (MacOS X, Windows, Linux.)

A.3.3　Treat yourself to PDFView

Use PDFView for viewing PDF files generated by LaTeX, it integrates tightly with your LaTeX text editor. PDFView is an open-source application, available from the PDFView website on `http://pdfview.sourceforge.net/`. After installing, open PDFViews preferences dialog and make sure that the *automatically reload documents* option is enabled and that PDFSync support is set appropriately.

A.4　TeX on Windows

A.4.1　Getting TeX

First, get a copy of the excellent MiKTeX distribution from `http://www.miktex.org/`. It contains all the basic programs and files required to compile LATEX documents. The coolest feature in my eyes, is that MiKTEX will download missing LATEX packages on the fly and install them magically while compiling a document. Alternatively you can also use the TeXlive distribution which exists for Windows, Unix and Mac OS to get your base setup going `http://www.tug.org/texlive/`.

A.4.2 A LATEX editor

If you are not happy with our crossplatform suggestion Texmaker (section A.2).

TeXnicCenter uses many concepts from the programming-world to provide a nice and efficient LATEX writing environment in Windows. Get your copy from
`http://www.texniccenter.org/`. TeXnicCenter integrates nicely with MiK-TeX.

Recent TEXLive distributions contain the TEXworks Editor `http://texworks.org/`. It supports Unicode and requires at least Windows XP.

A.4.3 Document Preview

You will most likely be using Yap for DVI preview as it gets installed with MikTeX. For PDF you may want to look at Sumatra PDF `http://blog.kowalczyk.info/software/sumatrapdf/`. I mention Sumatra PDF because it lets you jump from any position in the pdf document back into corresponding position in your source document.

A.4.4 Working with graphics

Working with high quality graphics in LATEX means that you have to use Encapsulated POSTSCRIPT (eps) or PDF as your picture format. The program that helps you deal with this is called GhostScript. You can get it, together with its own front-end GhostView, from `http://www.cs.wisc.edu/~ghost/`.

If you deal with bitmap graphics (photos and scanned material), you may want to have a look at the open source Photoshop alternative Gimp, available from `http://gimp-win.sourceforge.net/`.

A.5 T_EX on Linux

If you work with Linux, chances are high that LATEX is already installed on your system, or at least available on the installation source you used to setup. Use your package manager to install the following packages:

- texlive – the base TEX/LATEX setup.

- emacs (with AUCTeX) – an editor that integrates tightly with LaTeX through the add-on AUCTeX package.

- ghostscript – a POSTSCRIPT preview program.

- xpdf and acrobat – a PDF preview program.

- imagemagick – a free program for converting bitmap images.

- gimp – a free Photoshop look-a-like.

- inkscape – a free illustrator/corel draw look-a-like.

If you are looking for a more windows like graphical editing environment, check out Texmaker. See section A.2.

Most Linux distros insist on splitting up their TeX environments into a large number of optional packages, so if something is missing after your first install, go check again.

Bibliography

[1] Leslie Lamport. *LaTeX: A Document Preparation System*. Addison-Wesley, Reading, Massachusetts, second edition, 1994, ISBN 0-201-52983-1.

[2] Donald E. Knuth. *The TeXbook,* Volume A of *Computers and Typesetting*, Addison-Wesley, Reading, Massachusetts, second edition, 1984, ISBN 0-201-13448-9.

[3] Frank Mittelbach, Michel Goossens, Johannes Braams, David Carlisle, Chris Rowley. *The LaTeX Companion, (2nd Edition)*. Addison-Wesley, Reading, Massachusetts, 2004, ISBN 0-201-36299-6.

[4] Michel Goossens, Sebastian Rahtz and Frank Mittelbach. *The LaTeX Graphics Companion*. Addison-Wesley, Reading, Massachusetts, 1997, ISBN 0-201-85469-4.

[5] Each LaTeX installation should provide a so-called *LaTeX Local Guide*, which explains the things that are special to the local system. It should be contained in a file called `local.tex`. Unfortunately, some lazy sysops do not provide such a document. In this case, go and ask your local LaTeX guru for help.

[6] LaTeX3 Project Team. *LaTeX 2ε for authors*. Comes with the LaTeX 2ε distribution as `usrguide.tex`.

[7] LaTeX3 Project Team. *LaTeX 2ε for Class and Package writers*. Comes with the LaTeX 2ε distribution as `clsguide.tex`.

[8] LaTeX3 Project Team. *LaTeX 2ε Font selection*. Comes with the LaTeX 2ε distribution as `fntguide.tex`.

[9] D. P. Carlisle. *Packages in the 'graphics' bundle*. Comes with the 'graphics' bundle as `grfguide.tex`, available from the same source your LaTeX distribution came from.

[10] Rainer Schöpf, Bernd Raichle, Chris Rowley. *A New Implementation of LaTeX's verbatim Environments*. Comes with the 'tools' bundle as

`verbatim.dtx`, available from the same source your LaTeX distribution came from.

[11] Vladimir Volovich, Werner Lemberg and LaTeX3 Project Team. *Cyrillic languages support in LaTeX*. Comes with the LaTeX 2_ε distribution as `cyrguide.tex`.

[12] Graham Williams. *The TeX Catalogue* is a very complete listing of many TeX and LaTeX related packages. Available online from `CTAN: //help/Catalogue/catalogue.html`

[13] Keith Reckdahl. *Using EPS Graphics in LaTeX 2_ε Documents*, which explains everything and much more than you ever wanted to know about EPS files and their use in LaTeX documents. Available online from `CTAN://info/epslatex.ps`

[14] Kristoffer H. Rose. *XY-pic User's Guide*. Downloadable from CTAN with XY-pic distribution

[15] John D. Hobby. *A User's Manual for METAPOST*. Downloadable from `http://cm.bell-labs.com/who/hobby/`

[16] Alan Hoenig. *TeX Unbound*. Oxford University Press, 1998, ISBN 0-19-509685-1; 0-19-509686-X (pbk.)

[17] Urs Oswald. *Graphics in LaTeX 2_ε*, containing some Java source files for generating arbitrary circles and ellipses within the `picture` environment, and *METAPOST - A Tutorial*. Both downloadable from `http://www.ursoswald.ch`

[18] Till Tantau. *TikZ&PGF Manual*. Download from `CTAN://graphics/pgf/base/doc/generic/pgf/pgfmanual.pdf`

[19] François Charette. *Polyglossia: A Babel Replacement for XeLaTeX*. Comes with the TeXLive distribution as `polyglossia.pdf`. (Type `texdoc polyglossia` on the command line.)

[20] François Charette. *An ArabTeX-like interface for typesetting languages in Arabic script with XeLaTeX*. Comes with the TeXLive distribution as `arabxetex.pdf`. (Type `texdoc arabxetex` on the command line.)

[21] Will Robertson and Khaled Hosny. *The `fontspec` package*. Comes with the TeXLive distribution as `fontspec.pdf`. (Type `texdoc fontspec` on the command line.)

[22] Apostolos Syropoulos. *The `xgreek` package*. Comes with the TeXLive distribution as `xgreek.pdf`. (Type `texdoc xgreek` on the command line.)

[23] Vafa Khalighi. *The bidi package.* Comes with the TeXLive distribution as `bidi.pdf`. (Type `texdoc bidi` on the command line.

[24] Vafa Khalighi. *The XePersian package.* Comes with the TeXLive distribution as `xepersian-doc.pdf`. (Type `texdoc xepersian` on the command line.

[25] Wenchang Sun. *The xeCJK package.* Comes with the TeXLive distribution as `xeCJK.pdf`. (Type `texdoc xecjk` on the command line.

Index

Made in the USA
Lexington, KY
22 June 2018